CONTENTS

FOREWORD

'Housing for Single People, Shared Accommodation and Hostels' forms part of a series of documents known collectively as the **Scottish Housing Handbook.** In producing the Handbook, the aim is to look at problems comprehensively to ensure that the diverse housing needs of all sections of our society are met in the most effective and satisfactory way. For convenience, the Handbook is divided into separate parts and each part deals with a specific aspect of housing needs and provision.

Parts of the Handbook already published are as follows:

Part 1: 'Assessing Housing Needs: A Manual of Guidance' (published 1977)

Part 3: 'Housing Development: Layout, Roads and Services' (published 1977)

Part 5: 'Housing for the Elderly' (published 1980)

Part 6: 'Housing for the Disabled' (published 1979)

This part of the Handbook, Part 7, examines the need for housing for single people, and suggests ways of providing accommodation suitable for a variety of special needs of which the principal common feature is that the people involved are usually single. Design standards are proposed for a number of different types of housing, of which none is entirely new. They are either types for which no standards have previously been published or which have been published only in summary form, or else are alternative ways of using types of housing for which standards are already established. The introduction of housing designed to these standards should provide authorities with a more flexible range of accommodation and should help them to fill gaps in the housing stock to meet the needs of certain special groups which have hitherto been neglected.

The Scottish Housing Handbook is intended primarily for the use of public sector housing authorities in Scotland and their consultants, although it is hoped that the guidance may also be helpful to those working in the private sector. Officers of the Scottish Development Department are available to housing authorities and others for consultation on any subject covered by the Handbook.

Housing for Single People, Shared Accommodation and Hostels

Scottish Development Department
Her Majesty's Stationery Office

ISBN 0 11 492390 6

Housing for Single People, Shared Accommodation and Hostels

1.1 MAIN OBJECTIVES

1.1.1 The purpose of this part of the Handbook is to amplify the existing design standards for hostels, and to offer guidance on the design of other forms of housing for single people.

1.1.2 In Scotland previous design standards for housing for single people were based upon hostels as described in SDD Circular 10/1975. The standards in this circular were always intended merely to be a stop-gap measure until more was known about the needs of single people and experience had been gained of other types of accommodation. It is now clear that hostel standards are not suitable for all the various forms of communal living, and that there are types of shared accommodation which fall between housing and hostels, and which do not readily fit the description contained in the circular in either size or function.

1.1.3 During the last few years there has been a growing interest in the housing needs of single people. This has arisen partly through an increase in the number of single people of all ages wishing to live as independent one-person households. It is also related to the provision of accommodation for special needs and a concern for the plight of the single homeless.

1.1.4 In considering the 'needs' aspects of housing for single people (as covered in Chapter 2) and the design and standards aspects (as covered in Chapters 3 and 4) it is most important that full account should be taken of resource and cost implications. The discussion of needs in Chapter 2 implies that careful assessments will be made so that a balance can be struck between competing priorities for capital resources. Once a decision in principle has been made the project design and standards should take full account of economy, both of initial capital costs and subsequent running costs. Life-cycle costing techniques should be adopted to ensure that the new or adapted buildings are not unnecessarily costly to run or to maintain. Given a carefully balanced design initial capital costs need not be significantly affected on that account. It is particularly important that the lists of optional features at 4.2.2, 4.3.2 and 4.4.2 should be closely considered, and, so far as possible, the design team brief should define from the outset which, if any, of the optional features are required in a given case.

1.1.5 The guidance offered by SDD is intended to be of assistance to everyone involved in the provision of housing, in both public and private sectors, irrespective of the source of funding for individual schemes. At the same time the recommendations are neither exhaustive nor exclusive; they should be used as a framework in the formulation of flexible policies and programmes.

1.2 DEFINITIONS

1.2.1 The following definitions are intended solely to clarify the use of these terms in this Handbook. Definitions of rooms inside the dwelling should be taken as those contained in the Building Regulations.

1.2.2 Apartment—any habitable room, excluding kitchen, bathroom, WC, utility spaces, storage cupboards and circulation areas.

1.2.3 Dwelling—any self-contained place of residence including a house or flat.

1.2.4 House—a dwelling on one or more floors which is divided vertically from every other dwelling and has its principal access from ground level.

1.2.5 Flat—a dwelling on one floor, forming part of a building from some other part of which it is divided horizontally.

1.2.6 Family—a group closely connected by blood or affinity, normally consisting of parents and children, whether living together permanently or not.

1.2.7 Household—the occupants of a dwelling considered collectively, whether or not they are all of one family.

1.2.8 Mainstream dwelling—general needs house or flat intended for occupation by a group living as a single independent household and normally comprising the members of one family.

1.2.9 Water Closet—the term refers to the compartment and not the fitting.

1.2.10 Building Regulations—the Building Standards (Scotland) Regulations currently in force.

1.2.11 Metric Dimensions—linear dimensions on all diagrams are given in metres or millimetres. The following abbreviations are used:

m=metres   m²=square metres
mm=millimetres   m³=cubic metres

Housing for Single People, Shared Accommodation and Hostels

2.1 VARIOUS TYPES OF NEED

2.1.1 The decision to issue a separate part of the Handbook on housing for single people may suggest, at first sight, a wish to highlight the social characteristics of individuals who, for whatever reason, are not members of a conventional nuclear family. In fact the various forms of accommodation described cover a wide range of types of need, but the one common factor linking them all is the presupposition that the occupants will usually be single. It is felt that consideration of lifestyle is nowadays probably a more meaningful way of defining this group than marital status. The state of 'singleness' therefore is not in itself regarded as a special need but as the common characteristic of various types of need. Single people do not necessarily require special forms of housing and, in general terms, there is no particular reason why mainstream housing should not be suitable for most single person households. Neither is there any reason why a particular household should have special housing needs simply because of there being only one person in that household.

2.1.2 In the context of general needs housing it is more important to consider other ways in which mainstream dwellings could be used by single people either living on their own in one-person dwellings, or as part of a group sharing a family dwelling. Thus the whole range of normal mainstream dwellings may be appropriate in such circumstances although house allocation policies are crucial in determining levels of demand for accommodation for single people. Much depends upon intelligent use being made of the available housing stock (see 3.6.1).

2.1.3 The ultimate aim of most single people wishing to live independently is likely to be to occupy a dwelling of their own, just the same as any other type of household. Those who have established themselves in the community as single people will therefore most probably seek accommodation in small dwellings within the stock of general needs housing. This group is therefore identifiable only in the sense that there may be a shortage of appropriate dwellings (see 2.3) in the most favoured locations in any particular area (see 2.7).

2.1.4 An increasing number of young single people are seeking independent accommodation and this group is likely to require a variety of types of accommodation and forms of tenure. Many of them may be unable yet to afford the purchase or rent of an independent dwelling and they would be happy to share in the meantime a larger house or flat with a number of other like-minded individuals. Their situation is complicated by two additional factors. Firstly, their need for this form of accommodation may be relatively short-lived if, for instance, they wish to marry or form a lasting relationship with another individual and decide then to seek a dwelling of their own. Secondly, they may often not be able to stay in one place for any length of time because of changes in their occupation if, for instance, they cannot find suitable employment in the part of the country where their further education or training has taken place. For this reason the group have sometimes been referred to as 'young mobile' single people, and it is particularly the transient nature of their housing need which distinguishes it from other special needs or from general needs.

2.1.5 Accommodation for single people may also be relevant to other housing for special needs. Guidance on the design of dwellings for elderly or disabled people is included in Scottish Housing Handbook, Part 5: 'Housing for the Elderly' and Part 6: 'Housing for the Disabled'. These groups may also be catered for in certain other types of accommodation, particularly in situations where a higher than normal degree of care is being provided, where the occupants may be more frail and dependent, or where they have severe physical disabilities. The detailed design considerations advocated in those parts of the Handbook would therefore be applicable also to housing for single people intended for occupation by these groups (see 3.1.12, 3.5.32).

2.1.6 The mentally handicapped are another special needs group whose members are often single and for whom relatively little specific housing provision has been made in the past. Traditional forms of accommodation have generally been institutional in character. However it is now thought that a wide range of mentally handicapped people could benefit from a more domestic living environment within the community if appropriate support is provided. This type of accommodation might also be used to house groups of people recovering from mental illness. They require a range of housing provision involving single as well as shared tenancies and other forms of group living. A small number of housing associations in Scotland have already been active in promoting the housing of mentally handicapped people in relatively small groups with some degree of care provided by houseparents, wardens, or other residential or visiting staff.

Small hostel for special needs, of domestic scale and with warden's house attached.

Hostel for mentally handicapped people built around a small courtyard and incorporating some mainstream dwellings intended for families including a mentally handicapped person.

2.1.7 There are a number of other groups of single people who have special housing needs arising from mainly social, as opposed to physical or psychological circumstances. These are characterised by generally being very poor, having difficulty in managing their day to day lives, being unable to gain satisfactory or permanent employment, unwilling to commit themselves to living in one place for any length of time and, in some cases, by other factors such as alcoholism. Hostels will be suitable for many people in this situation, although there are various forms which the accommodation might take. The mobility of these groups also implies the possibility in many cases of eventually moving away from hostels towards the greater independence of general needs housing. The provision of a range of types of accommodation for single people is intended to enhance the opportunities for this. The same would apply to ex-offenders and young people leaving care. Both these groups could benefit from hostels or shared accommodation with a measure of support for at least a short time, although in most cases they would be capable eventually of moving into ordinary housing.

2.1.8 Finally, it is necessary to consider various other situations where accommodation broadly intended for single people might be used to provide relatively short term accommodation for those faced with a crisis in their lives. Included here would be homeless people, battered wives, divorcees, single-parent families, and others who may not be 'single' in the strict sense of the word.

2.1.9 The considerable range of types of need described in these paragraphs shows that there are many different forms of accommodation possible and that there are various ways of using them. It would clearly be impossible to prescribe a definitive solution for such diverse needs; this document points instead to a flexible range of solutions within the framework of three broad categories of housing.

2.2 NUMBER OF ONE-PERSON HOUSEHOLDS

2.2.1 Perhaps the most important reason for issuing guidance on this subject at present is the increase in the number of one-person households.

2.2.2 During the past 30 years, the number of one-person households (and their proportion of all households) has grown rapidly and is expected to continue to increase although possibly at a slower rate (see Table 1). In 1981, the number of one-person households in Scotland was 392,850 (22% of all households), and it is projected to rise to 482,300 (25% of all households) by 1991.

2.2.3 However the number of one-person households is still much less than the number of non-married adults—that is, single, widowed or divorced (see Table 2).

2.2.4 The first and perhaps most obvious reason for this difference is that many single people remain living with their parents into adulthood: they stay at home.

Housing for Single People, Shared Accommodation and Hostels

TABLE 1

ONE-PERSON PRIVATE HOUSEHOLDS

General Register Office for Scotland, Censuses 1951, 1961, 1971 and 1981
Scottish Household Projections (1979-based)

		1951[1]		1961[1]		1971[2]		1981[2]		1991	
		No.	%	No.	%	No.	%	No.	%	No.	%
One Person Households	15-ret	—	—	90,347	5.8	98,459	5.9	129,282	7.2	167,500	8.8
	ret+	—	—	130,344	8.3	202,320	12.0	263,568	14.8	314,800	16.5
	All 1p	159,966	11.1	220,691	14.1	300,779	17.9	392,850	22.0	482,300	25.3
All Households		1,435,925	100	1,569,817	100	1,681,216	100	1,785,936	100	1,903,500	100

[1] 1951 and 1961 as enumerated.

[2] 1971 and 1981 includes present and absent residents.

2.2.5 Secondly, single adult dependent relatives, for instance elderly parents or disabled siblings, live in households headed by members of their families. In addition a significant number of households consist of a lone parent with children, although the parent would be enumerated as single (or widowed or divorced) in the population figures. On the other hand the one-person household figures do include a small number of married people.

2.2.6 Thirdly, single people living in lodgings would be included in the one-person household figures only if they prepared all their meals themselves. Lodgers who have at least one meal per day provided for them are counted as part of the host household. Similarly groups of individuals sharing a dwelling voluntarily are only counted as independent one-person households if they each prepare all their own meals. Otherwise they would comprise a multi-person household. The situation of shared occupancies may be further complicated by the existence of one or more common-law marriages within the larger group, and a couple who were cohabiting would not be counted as two separate one-person households.

TABLE 2

SINGLE, WIDOWED AND DIVORCED PEOPLE IN THE ADULT (15+) PRIVATE HOUSEHOLD POPULATION

General Register Office for Scotland, Censuses 1951, 1961, 1971 and 1981
Scottish Household Projections (1979-based)

		1951[1]		1961[1]		1971[1]		1981		1991	
		No.	%	No.	%	No.	%	No.	%	No.	%
Single and Widowed/ Divorced	15-ret	1,231,397	32.1	1,057,197	27.5	976,741	25.2	1,073,832	27.7	997,600	25.7
	ret+	352,704	9.2	386,169	10.1	429,763	11.1	406,075	10.5	406,800	10.5
	All SWD	1,584,101	41.3	1,443,366	37.6	1,406,504	36.3	1,479,907	38.1	1,404,400	36.2
Total Pop 15+		3,831,956	100	3,840,246	100	3,839,939	100	3,881,094	100	3,880,900	100

[1] 1951, 1961 and 1971 includes non-private households.

TABLE 3

TENURE OF ONE-PERSON PRIVATE HOUSEHOLDS

General Register Office for Scotland, Censuses 1961, 1971 and 1981

	1961[1]		1971		1981	
	No.	%	No.	%	No.	%
Owner Occupied	61,060	27.7	87,101	29.1	113,906	29.2
Public Rented[2]	56,954	25.8	136,376	45.6	221,077	56.6
Private Rented[3]	102,677	46.5	75,889	25.3	55,531	14.2
All Tenures	220,691	100	299,366	100	390,514	100
Not Stated or Not In Permanent Accommodation	—	—	1,433	0.5	2,336	0.6

[1] Those listed as 'not stated' in 1961 are distributed between sectors on a *pro rata* basis.

[2] Public Rented includes local authorities, New Towns and SSHA.

[3] Private Rented includes housing associations, dwellings rented with a business or by virtue of employment, and unfurnished or furnished rented dwellings.

2.2.7 Fourthly, a significant number of single adults are enumerated as either residents or staff of non-private establishments (hotels, hostels, hospitals, nursing-homes, college residences, boarding schools, penal and defence establishments etc) and are not included in the population figures which relate to numbers of persons in private households.

2.2.8 It is therefore rather difficult to estimate accurately the number of people who are potential one-person households. Furthermore the level of demand for housing for single people and, indeed, the rate of one-person household formation, would be affected by the availability of suitable forms of accommodation in any particular area. Nevertheless, it would be reasonable to conclude that potential exists for the number of one-person households to increase beyond the projection of current trends, although it is most unlikely that in the foreseeable future social changes would cause the formation of one-person households to reach the total number of single people in the population.

2.3 SUPPLY OF HOUSING FOR SINGLE PEOPLE

2.3.1 Simultaneously with the marked increase in the number of single people living as independent one-person households, there has been a substantial decrease in supply of the forms of accommodation traditionally used to house them, particularly for young single people.

2.3.2 In 1981 only 33% of those enumerated in the census as one-person households were under pensionable age, whereas 73% of those listed as single, widowed or divorced in the population figures were between the ages of 15 and retirement. The shortage of suitable accommodation for single people is indeed most acute among the younger age groups, partly because owner occupation and public rental are not so readily available and, perhaps most importantly, because there has been a significant reduction in the size of the private rented sector (see Table 3).

2.3.3 The private rented sector has traditionally played an important role in meeting the needs of single people, principally because it has been more accessible than other types of accommodation. Therefore, reductions in the size of this sector have serious consequences for single people.

2.3.4 The decrease in the private sector's proportion of the housing stock has coincided with the growth of building for private sale. From a position of relative unimportance at the beginning of the century, owner occupation has increased to 35% of all households. On the other hand, only 30% of one-person households are in the owner occupied sector.

2.3.5 The emphasis in owner occupation has been mainly on family dwellings and the necessity for Building Societies to ensure regular mortgage repayments has generally resulted in preference being given to the secure family unit, headed by a man of working age in permanent salaried employment. On the other hand, the financial circumstances of young single people in many cases are such that they are unlikely to be considered for a Building Society loan, particularly if they have only a short or erratic employment record, or are self-employed or unsalaried.

2.3.6 The conditions for granting loans for property purchase are generally such that the property itself becomes the security on the loan. This results in the lender being concerned that the property will be easy to sell if the mortgage goes by default and this has caused Building Societies to be cautious about granting loans on older housing in city centres or on dwellings of unconventional form. Not only are young single people themselves at a disadvantage in the owner-occupied sector, but the type of accommodation most likely to be favoured by them is also difficult to obtain from this source. (The suitable form and location of development is discussed more fully in Section 2.7.)

2.3.7 Likewise until comparatively recently public funded housing programmes in some areas concentrated almost exclusively on three or four apartment family dwellings, although in the early seventies attention was turned to the provision of small dwellings for special needs, particularly for the elderly. However, for young single people of working age public rented housing has remained largely inaccessible. Where local authorities have operated a system of points for assessing the need of individual households on the waiting lists, single people have generally been accorded a very low priority.

2.4 SIMILAR TYPES OF ACCOMMODATION IN OTHER FIELDS

2.4.1 Throughout this part of the Handbook, emphasis is placed on the different ways in which housing may be used to cater for single people and upon other forms of accommodation broadly fulfilling the census and legal meaning of 'private dwelling'. In the foregoing statistical analysis (see 2.2 and 2.3) the figures refer only to households occupying dwellings so defined. However, in terms of function, a rather looser definition of housing is preferable and this would also include certain other types of residential accommodation. Brief reference has already been made (see 2.2.7) to single people living in non-private establishments, as they are called in the census. Some of these are useful as prototypes for forms of accommodation which could logically be included under the broad heading of housing and which are important in the context of single people and special needs groups.

2.4.2 Hostels are probably the most obviously analogous type. They are already often considered as a form of housing and they perform a valuable function in the provision of accommodation for many single people. The problem is that, as with private rented dwellings since the sixties, there has been a marked reduction in the number of available places.

2.4.3 In 1965 the then National Assistance Board made a survey of hostels and lodging houses owned by local authorities, charitable and voluntary bodies and commercial organisations, in Britain. Seven years later the office of Population Censuses and Surveys brought the information gleaned from the earlier survey up to date and the final confidential report was produced in 1975. The OPCS discovered that nearly half of the establishments surveyed in 1965 had closed down. The most common causes given for closure were: the property had been redeveloped; the business had ceased to be commercially viable; the proprietor had retired; or the local authority had judged the premises to be a health or fire hazard. Most of the buildings were very old and in Scotland three-quarters of the accommodation was in establishments which failed to meet the then current standards for provision of sanitary fittings.

2.4.4 A number of hostels have recently been built or modernised and some housing associations and other agencies are becoming increasingly active in providing small hostels or similar types of accommodation for special needs groups in both new and adapted buildings.

Hostels perform a valuable function in the provision of accommodation for some sections of the community.

Universities often provide accommodation for students in the form of hostels, sometimes grouped together on a campus.

2.4.5 A significant number of young single people are students. For many years universities, colleges and other places of higher education have provided residential accommodation for those attending full-time courses. This has generally taken the form of hostels grouped together on a campus, or sometimes in large specially converted houses. Although these would be classed as non-private establishments, there can be little doubt that they are fulfilling a housing function and it is therefore useful to see them as examples of those types of accommodation.

2.4.6 The private rented sector also has provided short or medium term housing for students wishing to share. Tenement flats in the older urban areas have proved suitable for this purpose: prices are low and there is a relatively rapid turnover combined with easy accessibility. These properties also have the advantage of being close to the city centres, college buildings, shops, places of entertainment and other facilities considered important by single people. The form of tenure also relieves the occupants of responsibility for maintenance. From the point of view of the landlord the student social network ensures that vacancies are readily filled by friends of the tenant group. The limited timescale in higher education enables the landlord to relet or sell at the end of each academic year, or at least when the group of students reach the end of their courses and move away or set up house on their own.

Many students occupy shared accommodation in the private rented sector, frequently in tenement flats close to the city centre and main college buildings.

Housing for Single People, Shared Accommodation and Hostels

A number of health boards now provide accommodation for nurses and other staff in the form of shared houses or flats.

2.4.7 In recent years some universities have provided accommodation in the form of cluster flats, either newly-built or in converted tenements. This has gone some way towards filling the gap left by the shrinking private rented sector. This is advantageous for the students, as they are provided with purpose-designed study-bedrooms in place of the somewhat makeshift arrangements in private rented flats where rooms are often shared and unsuitably furnished. In some cases colleges have rented houses or flats from private landlords or housing authorities and, acting as a main tenant, they have used them to accommodate groups of students on sub-letting agreements. This arrangement can be beneficial for the students in that the college is more likely to be able to persuade landlords to carry out essential repairs timeously and to negotiate appropriate levels of rent on their behalf. On the other hand the landlord is less likely to encounter problems over collecting rent. A steady income is ensured and he does not have to concern himself with advertising or letting.

2.4.8 Similar types of residential accommodation are provided for nursing, medical and other staff in hospitals. In the past a measure of supervision was considered necessary for the younger staff including student nurses, who were required to live in traditional nurses' homes. The occupants of hostels of this type generally now enjoy a much higher level of freedom and in many establishments the sexes are no longer segregated. As with students, the private rented sector also has traditionally provided accommodation for nurses, and recently a number of health authorities have used slightly modified standard house shells for nurses homes. New developments generally take this form.

2.4.9 Other areas to which one might look for examples are the types of accommodation used by single servicemen or prison officers, and of particular interest recently with the growth of oil-related industries, temporary or short-term housing for migrant or itinerant workers. Thus, the standards for housing for single people proposed in this part of the Handbook, for which there are already close parallels in other fields, may have some relevance across a broad spectrum of needs.

2.5 FUNCTIONAL REQUIREMENTS OF DIFFERENT CATEGORIES

2.5.1 The aspirations and needs of adult single people are probably more diverse and less widely understood than those of people in traditional family situations and their ability to afford the cost of suitable housing is extremely variable. The provision and management of accommodation should reflect this diversity, and should seek to introduce a variety of types of housing which may be flexible in application and use, sympathetic to existing differences in domestic arrangements and responsive to new patterns of living. Above all, the profile of the housing stock and the forms of accommodation available should provide scope for choice. This is obviously the ideal situation in the longer term, but those people who are charged with providing accommodation for all groups will also need to be realistic about what can be achieved in the short term.

2.5.2 One of the most significant factors in the selection of suitable forms of development for single people is the degree to which the occupants are expected to live independently. In terms of the basic functions of housing, it is assumed that everyone needs somewhere private to sleep and store a limited quantity of personal belongings. The extent to which living space, sanitary and bathing facilities and catering areas are also required privately for each household may vary from total independence on the one hand to completely communal living on the other. Between these two extremes lie various degrees of sharing and many different ways of providing the accommodation.

2.5.3 For the sake of simplifying the briefing process and scheme design, it is proposed to divide the broad spectrum described above into three distinct categories of housing. These are *One-Person Housing, Shared Housing* and *Hostels*. It may be helpful to take each of these categories in turn and to consider their definitions in terms of distinctive features and functional requirements.

Private space is required for sleeping and for storing personal belongings; the other housing functions may, to a greater or lesser extent, be shared with others.

One-person Housing: flatted development incorporating a large proportion of one-person dwellings.

Shared Housing: development consisting of terraced houses and flats.

Hostel: small scheme including a hostel for 10 residents and a warden's house.

One-Person Housing

2.5.4 This would be ordinary mainstream dwellings designed for occupation by a single person.

2.5.5 Occupants would generally be people who had reached a relatively settled period in their lives and who wish to set up house on a secure and permanent basis.

2.5.6 The level of supervision would not exceed the normal housing management functions.

2.5.7 Occupants would be completely independent in the organisation of their day to day living.

2.5.8 The accommodation would consist of an independent dwelling for each person, containing either a single bedroom and living room, or a large bed-sitting room, together with kitchen, bathroom and storage space all for the exclusive use of the occupant. Each dwelling would be separate in the sense of having its own front door to the outside or onto the common access stair or corridor in a block of flats.

Shared Housing

2.5.9 This would be similar to mainstream dwellings, and would be intended for occupation by a group of individuals who are usually unrelated. The number of people residing in each dwelling would be no more than the range normally encountered in a single family household ie 2–8, although the range 4–6 is likely to be common.

2.5.10 The occupation of a dwelling by a group would generally be on a relatively permanent basis, although within the group one may expect a rapid turnover of individuals.

2.5.11 The members of the household would be independent in the organisation of their lives, either individually or as a group, with minimal external supervision or management in most cases.

2.5.12 They would be free to choose the extent to which they share or allocate responsibility for preparing meals and for other household chores. Thus to some extent they would be dependent upon one another, or 'interdependent'.

2.5.13 The accommodation would consist of a self-contained dwelling for each group, normally containing a study-bedroom for the private use of each person, together with shared living space, kitchen, sanitary accommodation and storage, for the exclusive use of the occupants of the dwelling collectively. As with one-person housing, the dwelling would be separate from any other dwellings, with its own front door opening to the outside, the common access stair or a corridor in a block of flats.

Hostels

2.5.14 This form of residential accommodation is intended for occupation by a group of unrelated individuals normally larger in number than that encountered in mainstream dwellings. It is likely that hostels in the range 10–50 will be preferred although in some exceptional cases accommodation for smaller or larger numbers might function as a hostel. Likewise the physical size of the accommodation would normally be beyond what could be regarded as a single dwelling.

2.5.15 In some instances occupants might use the accommodation on a relatively permanent basis. In general, however, most occupants' demand for accommodation would be of a more fluctuating nature than is normal in general needs housing.

2.5.16 This type of accommodation normally presupposes a degree of dependence upon communally provided services which sometimes involves an element of care or supervision.

2.5.17 Certain types of hostels might arrange for residents to cater for themselves. However it is more usual for at least one main meal to be provided each day, and for the size and organisation of the building to require a level of staffing capable of sustaining such a service for all residents together.

2.5.18 The accommodation normally would consist of a bed-sitting room for the private use of each resident, shared living rooms, dining rooms, sanitary accommodation and storage, with a kitchen, laundry and other ancillary accommodation appropriate to the provision of communal services. Typically a hostel would be designed as a single entity with corridors linking different parts of the building at each floor level, and with an identifiable (and possibly supervised) main entrance.

Combinations of Different Types

2.5.19 There are of course a number of options in between or straddling these categories, and various combinations might be envisaged for particular cases. For instance, design proposals could involve features drawn from more than one category in different parts of a large scheme, or housing for single people might be incorporated into schemes of predominantly general needs dwellings. It could also be built alongside housing for other special needs, although planning to meet possible variations in personal circumstances is necessary in the provision of accommodation for special needs just as it is more generally. It may be more important in some circumstances to provide normal housing in a particular location so as to be near a job, day centre or nursery, relative or friend, rather than providing a special type of accommodation.

2.6 MANAGEMENT, VALUATION, PLANNING AND BUILDING CONTROL ISSUES

2.6.1 In the foregoing paragraphs the three main categories of housing for single people were described in terms of their functions. Various other terms commonly used to describe forms of accommodation falling into one or other of these categories are listed in Table 4 together with the functional requirements. One of the main aims of the Scottish Housing Handbook is to describe various types of accommodation and to define them in terms of their physical characteristics by establishing appropriate standards of space, amenity and equipment. The design of the different types of housing for single people is discussed in Chapter 3 and is summarised in the checklist of recommended standards in Chapter 4. There are a number of other criteria where the distinction between dwellings (whether for one-person or multi-person households) and hostels is particularly significant. These functional matters are listed in Table 4.

2.6.2 In each case, in deciding which category should be applied to a particular type of building or form of accommodation, much hangs upon the meanings ascribed to the words 'dwelling' and 'household'. A more general definition of 'dwelling' would include any structure which has been built or adapted for the purpose of human habitation and which is wholly or mainly used as residential accommodation by the occupying household, irrespective of whether the occupation is by ownership or tenancy, exclusive or shared. By taking the word 'household' to mean the occupants of a dwelling whether they are members of a single family or an equivalent number of unrelated individuals, it becomes apparent that the occupants of a shared dwelling should be regarded as a single household, whereas in hostels it would clearly be inappropriate to consider the occupants in this way because of the size and functions of this type of accommodation.

2.6.3 Thus a house or flat occupied by a household so defined should always be regarded as a separate dwelling, and in situations where several one-person dwellings or shared dwellings are built as a terrace of houses or a block of flats, they should continue to be recognised as independent dwellings rather than being grouped and called a hostel.

Form of Tenancy

2.6.4 The significance of the split between the private and shared parts of the accommodation is clearly seen in relation to the different letting procedures and tenancy arrangements. The most common form is the joint and several liability agreement whereby each tenant of a shared property has total rights and responsibilities. The tenants are

TABLE 4

FUNCTIONS OF DIFFERENT TYPES OF ACCOMMODATION FOR SINGLE PEOPLE

Type	One-Person Housing	Shared Housing	Hostels
Other Terms in Common Usage	Single Person Dwellings Bed/Sit Dwellings Studio Flats One Bedroomed Houses Grouped Flatlets Sheltered Housing	Shared Mainstream Dwellings Small Group Homes (without staff) Cluster Flats Half-way Houses Follow-on Houses	Group Homes (with staff) Caring Hostels Community Houses Therapeutic Communities Supported Houses Hostel for ... (various client groups) Home for ... (various client groups) Lodging Houses Halls of Residence Boarding Houses Hotels
Number of Occupants	1	2–8 (4–6 preferred)	Rarely less than 10 and may be up to 50 or more
Nature of Occupation	Permanent/Settled	Relatively Permanent Groups (but may be turnover of individuals within groups)	Generally more Fluctuating (in character and extent; individuals may vary from permanent to short stay)
Level of Care or Supervision	None	Possibly external care or Supervision	Normally Resident Warden and/or Visiting Staff
Catering Arrangements	Fully Independent Self-Catering	Interdependent but Self-Catering (separately or communal)	Partially Dependent, Normally Catering Service (but can be self-catering or a mixture of both)
Nature of Accommodation	Self-Contained Dwelling	Study-Bedrooms (grouped together in a dwelling)	Bed-Sitting Rooms (within accommodation considered as a single entity and having a main entrance)
Form of Tenancy	Sole Tenancy	Joint and Several or Separate or Sub-let	'Right to Occupy'
Allocations	Housing List	Housing List plus Self-Selection	Separate List(s) or Referrals
Valuation and Rating	Domestic	Domestic	Non-Domestic (but may be eligible for Rating Relief)
Planning Use	Residential Single Occupation	Residential Single Occupation	Residential Multiple-Occupation
Building Control Classification	A1 or A2	A1 or A2	A3 (might be A4 in some cases)
Registration	—	—	Might be Registrable under Social Work or Public Health or Health Service Legislation

Housing for Single People, Shared Accommodation and Hostels

liable jointly for the rent and for damage to the property, but generally have control over the selection of new tenants and, to a great extent, tend to be self-managing as a group. This arrangement is considered by many to be the most suitable for shared dwellings where the tenants would be most likely to live as a group. Typically there is a high turnover of individual tenants but a lower turnover of groups. No risk is presented or specific problems posed by this arrangement and it has certain advantages for both landlord and tenants.

2.6.5 The other principal way tenancies are created is for separate tenancy agreements to be issued for each individual occupier. Each tenant has exclusive rights and responsibilities over his/her part of the property together with associated rights to use shared or communal areas. This arrangement would be particularly advantageous for tenants wishing short stay or temporary accommodation, or in situations where there may be too high a turnover of occupiers for group stability to emerge. It is likely to involve a greater management input, especially if the groups to be housed are not self-selected.

2.6.6 A third, less common arrangement is for the property to be let to a main tenant having permission to sub-let. It is thought that this would be unlikely to be popular with individual groups as it may place undue responsibility upon the signatory of the agreement and also would give sub-tenants few legal rights. There are some situations where it may be appropriate, for instance where mainstream dwellings are let to an educational establishment and sub-let to students, or where a hostel intended for a dependent special needs group can be let to a voluntary body or house parent as a main tenant. One-person dwellings could also be let in this way, although it would be more normal for the occupier to be the sole tenant.

2.6.7 In many hostels occupants have a 'right to occupy' rather than a tenancy as such, and the foregoing discussion would not be relevant to such hostels.

Allocations

2.6.8 The differences in function also affect the manner in which accommodation is allocated, the main distinction being between accommodation intended for individuals and that intended for sharing groups. Selection of tenants for single person dwellings should pose no particular problem and can usually be carried out according to the same rules as are applied to other applicants. Housing agencies introducing provision for single people for the first time may find that they need to publicise the fact until the availability of such lettings becomes widely known, although experience has indicated that even

quite small scale advertising is likely to elicit an overwhelming response.

2.6.9 A different approach is necessary for letting to groups of single people wishing to share, whether the dwellings to be allocated are purpose built cluster flats or existing mainstream dwellings that a housing agency wishes to turn over to use by single people. It is of course essential for each house to be occupied by people who are likely to be able to live together as a household. To achieve this there are two distinct parts of the letting process to be considered: the initial formation of a group and the allocation of a vacant house to it; and the selection of replacements for people leaving existing groups. Contrary to popular belief, groups of friends do not necessarily make successful 'flatmates'. In practice it has been found that strangers who have come together specifically for the purpose of sharing are the most satisfactory. However it would be reasonable to permit existing groups to choose their own replacements for vacancies. In both processes the housing agency may play an active role by, for instance, circulating lists of people interested in sharing, arranging meetings for such people, or nominating applicants for vacancies when requested. The agency may feel that it is necessary to restrict tenants to those who would qualify for its waiting list, or to reserve a right of veto, but an unduly restrictive attitude is likely to be self-defeating. It is unlikely that an agency's existing allocation system will be of much relevance, either for selecting groups or individuals for replacements, and the introduction of a policy of providing housing for single people will generally require special arrangements to be made for such allocations.

2.6.10 Whatever method of allocation is used, it is important to consider the reasonableness of any waiting periods involved. We have seen that for many people the need for single person accommodation is transitory in nature and housing rationed through a long waiting list would be useless for such people. Provided a proper assessment of housing needs has been made, and provided there is sufficient housing available which is suitable for occupation by single people or groups wishing to share, there should be few problems. Where there is excess demand, single people should not be accorded any lower priority than other types of need.

Tenancy Qualifications

2.6.11 One of the most difficult questions relating to allocations and tenancy agreements is to decide the best manner of operating tenancy qualifications. We have already seen that there may be some circumstances when it is desirable to let the accommodation to groups who are not strictly speaking single persons. In addition we need to consider what happens when occupiers, for whatever reason, no longer fulfil the tenancy qualifications. For instance they may cease to be single, start to cohabit, get married; they may no longer be students, nurses, or other agreed special groups; or they may not be young or new to the area, when the accommodation was intended for young single people or incoming workers. It is obviously desirable to avoid possible overcrowding or diminution of the single person housing stock, and some tenants in these circumstances may themselves request a transfer into mainstream housing. Some authorities may fear exploitation of a lenient transfer system by people attempting to jump the waiting list for family dwellings in this way. It is hoped that a reasonably flexible attitude may be adopted so as to minimise hardship, and this also applies to situations where remaining tenants may be left responsible for payment of rent for vacancies created by absconding flatmates, and who may wish to transfer as a result.

Valuation and Rating

2.6.12 Another important distinction between housing and hostels arises in the different ways in which they are valued for the purpose of assessing local authority rates payments. Responsibility for deciding which valuation category should be applied to the property in question rests with the Regional Assessors. A recent order made by the Secretary of State is designed to ensure that property akin to dwelling-houses, shared by single people, which has sometimes been valued on a commercial basis, will in future always be valued on a domestic basis. Thus, one-person dwellings and shared dwellings should normally be valued as domestic subjects, and hostels as non-domestic.

2.6.13 For valuation purposes the classification of a building as a hostel may result in a higher level of rates per tenant than if the accommodation had been classed as comprising individual dwellings. In many cases, however, hostels will be eligible for rating relief either on account of the type of resident to be catered for (eg disabled) or because of the nature of the building owner's or manager's organisation (eg charitable status). Such rating relief can reduce substantially the actual amount payable.

Planning

2.6.14 It is necessary also to consider how the different types of accommodation would be treated in planning terms. In general, all the categories should be regarded as residential in character and thus subject to the planning considerations governing residential development generally. In certain cases a special needs hostel might be regarded as a residential home and in these circumstances, parti-

cularly where it was proposed to occupy an existing house for this purpose, a material change of use would be involved. The question of differentiating between single and multiple occupation under planning legislation also arises. It would seem appropriate for shared dwellings to be treated as single occupation because this type of occupation corresponds closely to normal housing in size and function. On the other hand, in a number of respects the size and function of hostels is significantly different from normal housing and it is therefore appropriate that they should be considered as 'multiple occupation'.

Building Control

2.6.15 Buildings are classified by statute into different occupancy groups. Owing to the variations that may occur in the precise nature of individual developments or the mix of different types of accommodation, it is impossible to recommend specific occupancy groupings. In any case, the question of classification in particular instances would be the responsibility of the local authority building control department. As a general guide it would be appropriate for single person dwellings and shared dwellings to be classified as A1 or A2 (ie as houses or flats), and for hostels to be classified A3. If a building was intended to house very frail and dependent elderly, or severely handicapped people, it might be classified A4 (ie as a special needs home) although that situation would probably be rare in the context of housing provision. In addition, where a substantial part of the building is given over to a particular use, this might be considered separately. For instance, if a common room was included in a block of flats that room should be designed in accordance with the C2 classification (ie as an assembly or meeting space) as is the case in sheltered housing, although this would not apply to communal living or dining areas within each shared dwelling.

2.6.16 The main reason for having occupancy groups in the building regulations is to identify appropriate fire protection and escape requirements. For this the degree of dependence of the occupants and the extent of supervision or management are highly relevant, and these may vary considerably from scheme to scheme and over time. The differences in precise functions between the various types of shared accommodation for single people can be rather fine although the implications of different occupancy groups are nevertheless very significant, in terms of enclosed stairs, alternative escape routes, fire detection systems, smoke dispersal arrangements, and other cost-additive or restrictive features in the design or layout of the buildings. It is thus essential that early consultations regarding any proposals involving these types of accommodation are held with the local authority building control officer in order to establish the particular requirements of an individual building project.

Other Authorities and Agencies

2.6.17 In addition to the foregoing distinctions between categories, it is important to stress the need for providers of housing to co-ordinate their activities with those of other authorities or agencies who may be involved in the care or support of the occupants. For instance, in the context of accommodation for special needs this would apply to Health Boards and Social Work Departments, particularly in situations where joint-funding of caring hostels is contemplated.

2.6.18 Certain authorities, agencies or voluntary bodies may also be providing accommodation closely resembling shared housing or hostels, for instance, under Social Work, Education or Health Service Legislation (see 2.4). It is therefore hoped that the guidance contained in this part of the Handbook may have some relevance beyond purely housing interests.

2.7 LOCATION, SIZE AND TYPE OF DEVELOPMENT

2.7.1. Although the cost of accommodation is of paramount importance to young single people, its location also is often of considerable significance. For single people of working age, the patterns of daily living are not firmly focussed on the home: they are likely to be linked with a range of outside interests, such as places of employment, study, leisure and recreation, cultural and entertainment facilities and transportation.

2.7.2 Groups with particular needs, such as disabled single people, have other requirements, notably level access and proximity to bus stops, shops and other local facilities. These special problems are discussed more fully in Scottish Housing Handbook, Part 6. Otherwise, the exact siting of the building is not crucially important for single people, although it is obviously desirable that the new housing should be part of an existing community and that shops, cafes and pubs should be available nearby. It is also useful if shops in the area stay open late, although in practice there are many single people, for instance nurses and other shift-workers who keep irregular hours, for whom normal shop-opening times would not be such a problem.

2.7.3 Housing for single people can be provided in many different ways and with a variety of possible planning approaches ranging from single dwellings up to large self-contained housing developments. A substantial number of units would be required to support a variety of communal facilities, but the introduction of a very large development to an existing housing area can cause disruption in the social structure. Planning authorities are unlikely to favour proposals which might result in high concen-

trations of particular types of people in any one area, especially at high densities (see 2.6.14). On the whole it will be only in cities that very large schemes of exclusively single person housing will be either necessary or desirable. In other situations, developments of a smaller scale would be more appropriate. In many cases it may therefore be preferable to introduce single persons' housing in a large scheme of predominantly mainstream dwellings. Alternatively new housing could be built on a more piecemeal basis in gap sites or as part of rehabilitation schemes. Small projects of this size are unlikely to include communal facilities unless these were related to the housing area as a whole. In an established community, many of the facilities will already be available nearby and for the purposes of social integration it is undoubtedly preferable for incomers to be encouraged to use these rather than facilities relating only to the new housing.

2.7.4 The provision of a wide variety of accommodation requires the brief for each development to be thoroughly researched to obtain a clear understanding of the special needs of each group. Close co-operation between housing and social work authorities is vital to the success of many schemes especially where care of residents is involved, and between housing and education authorities where a large student population is to be accommodated.

Housing for single people can be provided in buildings similar to mainstream dwellings taking the form of houses or flats.

2.8 USING EXISTING BUILDINGS

2.8.1 In addition to specially designed new-build schemes, a major contribution to the stock of accommodation for small households is likely to come from the renovation or conversion of existing housing and other types of buildings. More detailed information is included in Section 3.6.

Pre-1919 Housing Stock

2.8.2. The traditional forms of accommodation for single people, particularly hostels, are mainly located in old buildings generally situated in urban

Upgrading of existing older buildings can provide opportunities for improving the living conditions of certain groups of single people occupying traditional types of hostels or shared accommodation.

areas (see 2.4.3). Many of these older properties are in poor condition with inadequate provision of sanitary accommodation and a low standard of basic living/sleeping space. Nevertheless they are still performing the essential function of providing short or medium term accommodation for certain groups of single people, particularly the single homeless and transient workers. In many instances such hostels will be retained, but conditions may be improved by additional shared facilities or by splitting up those hostels which contain large dormitories into smaller units of basic living space in order to provide more privacy and greater comfort and convenience for the occupants.

2.8.3 Many of the smaller hostels are conversions of existing dwellings. In areas around city centres

there are often excellent opportunities for providing accommodation for single people in old houses, some of which are too large for modern family living but nevertheless suitable for the number of occupants in a small hostel.

Large nineteenth century houses may be suitable for conversion to small hostels.

In some cases, it may be possible to provide accommodation for single people by altering and extending existing houses.

Housing for Single People, Shared Accommodation and Hostels

2.8.4 It is particularly desirable for young single people to be housed within easy reach of all the facilities available in urban areas (see 2.7.1). In the past, single people have often found accommodation in the private rented sector. This accommodation is frequently near city centres and in dwellings which have become unsuitable for families due to the noise and danger from heavy road traffic and possibly the shortage of private open space for children to play safely. The use of adaptations can help to maintain communities already weakened by dwellings falling empty and which would have become further dislocated by demolition and redevelopment.

Inter-War and Post-War Housing

2.8.5 During the seventies and eighties local authorities and other public-funded housing agencies have been active in improving the older housing stock. Much of this stock has reached the stage when it is desirable to carry out some improvement and repair works. The standard of facilities within the dwellings, particularly in the kitchens and bathrooms, is seen to be inadequate to satisfy the current aspirations of occupiers. Local authorities have therefore been concerned to maintain this important part of the housing stock by carrying out extensive programmes of modernisation and, especially in some of the more deprived areas, associated environmental improvements.

2.8.6 In improvement programmes there may be the possibility of 'opportunity conversions', ie the conversion of general needs housing to special needs. Perhaps the greatest advantage to be gained from using adapted mainstream dwellings to provide housing for special needs groups, for instance the mentally handicapped, is that the occupants will receive a stronger impression of being part of an existing community than they would if their accommodation had been purpose-built. In order to achieve the effective integration of special needs groups into the community, it is essential that they should not be stigmatised by having to live in buildings whose design is institutional in character. Ideally the accommodation should look as much like normal housing as possible. One way of achieving this is for the accommodation to be formed by joining together units that either have been or still are actual dwellings.

2.8.7 Some building forms lend themselves well to conversions of this nature. One of the building forms commonly used in the inter-war period, and one which would be particularly suitable for conversion to small hostels because of its size, is the four-in-a-block flatted type.

Older tenement flats are often rented by groups of single people, who may value highly the convenient locations often associated with this type of building.

Improvement programmes may provide opportunities for adapting more recent flatted accommodation to use by single people.

High-rise buildings are generally not favoured by families with young children but may nevertheless have a continuing useful life in the housing of single people.

High-Rise Development

2.8.8 During the sixties, much of the new public-funded housing took the form of multi-storey blocks of flats, sometimes on the edge of the cities but also in redeveloped housing sites around city centres.

2.8.9 Although the dwellings themselves were generally rather better equipped than those they had replaced, difficulties have often been encountered with lifts and public circulation areas. The problems of access to flats on upper storeys are particularly severe for families with young children where it is difficult for parents to maintain surveillance of play areas at ground level. In many cases this results in children being virtually confined to the dwellings. For this reason some local authorities are now pursuing a conscious policy of rehousing families at or near to ground floor level.

2.8.10 Although it is now generally recognised that multi-storey blocks are in some ways unsatisfactory for family living, there are certain groups for whom they would be well-suited. For instance, many young single people would be unlikely to find the lack of private open space unacceptable, and some might regard the distance from ground level as a positive advantage for privacy, outlook and security. A few examples already exist of multi-storey schemes purpose-built to cater for single people and this

Rehabilitation of older buildings to create shared dwellings provides opportunities for retention of important elements in the urban fabric.

Housing for Single People, Shared Accommodation and Hostels

seems to have been a successful solution which could be applied equally well to converted high-rise buildings. In conversions it would be desirable to have rather more communal facilities than is usual for mainstream housing, especially full-time caretaker services to maintain surveillance of main entrances and to supervise cleaning, repairs, deliveries and other communally provided services (see 3.3.15).

Other Types of Building

2.8.11   In addition to rehabilitating older housing, interest has been growing in the conversion and re-use of other building types. A major source of such buildings occurs in parts of towns where there has been commerce or industries which have moved elsewhere, or have ceased to function.

Urban Regeneration

2.8.12   The re-use of existing housing and other types of older buildings can thus play an important part in supplying the various forms of housing for single people. Conversions and adaptations provide opportunities for integrating the housing into existing communities. This is particularly advantageous for some special needs groups. When schemes of this type are carried out sensitively and complemented by the addition of appropriate new buildings on gap sites, they can greatly assist in the regeneration of run down parts of our towns and cities.

Conversions or adaptations can help to integrate housing for single people into existing communities and may contribute to the process of urban regeneration.

Housing for Single People, Shared Accommodation and Hostels

3.1 GENERAL DESCRIPTION

3.1.1 This Chapter gives design standards for all three categories of accommodation for single people: *One-Person Housing, Shared Housing,* and *Hostels.*

Private Accommodation

3.1.2 The three categories can be described by reference to the split between the 'private' domain and the 'shared' portions of the accommodation (see 2.5). General needs housing is usually regarded as comprising a number of individual, complete dwellings each fulfilling all the functions of housing and normally occupied by one household. One-person dwellings would be no different. In other words, the whole dwelling would be private accommodation.

However, in shared housing and hostels the basic unit of private accommodation is much smaller: it is either a bedroom, study-bedroom or bed-sitting room (see 3.4.6). It fulfils only the functions of sleeping, storing clothes and personal effects, and possibly studying, sitting and washing. All the other housing functions would be fulfilled by the use of shared accommodation.

Shared Accommodation

3.1.3 In shared housing and hostels, the gross floor area occupied by shared facilities covers all the functions that would be fulfilled in general needs housing by the living room, dining area, kitchen, bathroom and WC, general and linen storage, internal circulation and partitions.

TABLE 5

RECOMMENDED SPACE STANDARDS FOR ONE-PERSON HOUSING AND SHARED HOUSING

Purpose-Designed Dwellings

No. of Single Persons	1 (1 Apt)	1 (2 Apt)	2	3	4	5	6	7	8
Gross Area—m²/Person	33.0	37.0	28.7	25.9	23.7	22.0	20.7	19.7	18.9
Total Area—m²	33.0	37.0	57.4	77.7	94.8	110.0	124.2	137.9	151.2

Using Existing Mainstream Dwellings

No. of Single Persons	1	1	2	3	4	5	6
No. of Apartments	1	2	3	4	5	6	7
No. of Bedspaces[1] (Bulletin 1)	1	1/2	2/3/4	4/5/6[2]	5/6	7	8[3]
Gross Area Range—m² (Bulletin 1)	32.5–33.0	32.5–48.5	47.5–79.0	71.5–97.0	80.0–102.5	111.5–118.5	122.0–129.0

[1] Bedspaces per dwelling and floor areas are derived from New Scottish Housing Handbook, Bulletin 1: 'Metric Space Standards'.

[2] The areas for 4 apartment mainstream dwellings do not include 3 storey houses.

[3] Notional areas only are given for the 8 person house which was not included in Bulletin 1.

TABLE 6

RECOMMENDED SPACE STANDARDS FOR HOSTELS

No. of Residents	10	15	20	25	30	40	50	75	100
Gross Area—m²/Person	34.6	31.9	29.8	28.2	27.0	25.4	24.3	22.7	22.0
Total Area—m²	346	478.5	596	705	810	1,016	1,215	1,702.5	2,200

Space Standards

3.1.4 Recommended minimum space standards of one-person housing and shared housing are given in Table 5. The table also shows the various types of existing mainstream dwellings which might be chosen to house each number of single people. Recommended minimum space standards for hostels are given in Table 6. Intermediate sizes of hostel falling between points in the table can be obtained by interpolation.

3.1.5 In practice, there is scope for altering the exact apportionment of accommodation between the private and shared parts of a scheme (see 3.4.5), and account also needs to be taken of the effect upon the floor areas which the size of the scheme might have. Thus, the recommended space standards for shared housing and hostels given in Tables 5 and 6 are graduated in such a way that in each case the area per person decreases as the number of occupants increases across the range.

3.1.6 Gross floor areas are expressed in square metres per person, areas being measured between the internal faces of external walls. The areas are intended to cover all the items listed as essential in the summary of standards at Chapter 4.

3.1.7 Gross floor area comprises 'usable' and 'non-usable' areas. 'Non-usable' area covers partitions, ducts, staircases, entrance halls, lobbies, corridors and passages.

3.1.8 In one-person dwellings non-usable area is expected to be no more than about 17% of the gross floor area, or 20% of the 'usable' space. In shared dwellings these percentages would increase to about 20% and 25% respectively.

3.1.9 Where one-person or shared dwellings are provided in multi-storey blocks of flats, the area occupied by common access stairs, and by lifts and associated lobby space on each floor, would be additional to the gross floor area and thus is not included in the proportions indicated above.

3.1.10 In hostels, non-usable area may be expected to be about 25% of the gross floor area or 33% of the usable area. It is important to note that the part of this area which is used for circulation should meet all the requirements of the Building Regulations with regard to means of access and escape, the provision of corridors, staircases and where necessary lifts, fire-doors and exits. The choice of materials and fittings should be in accordance with those requirements (see 2.6.15).

Ancillary Accommodation and Optional Facilities

3.1.11 In addition to the basic units of private and shared accommodation, which together fulfil all the functions normally associated with general needs dwellings, there are certain other features of housing for single people which arise because of the large number of people to be accommodated, or because of the special needs of occupants. In considering the need for ancillary accommodation and optional facilities, additional to the basic accommodation, due regard should be paid to the costs involved, the possible extent of usage and any extra revenues likely to be received. Various types of spaces which might be necessary are discussed in more detail in later sections and they are listed as optional additional facilities in the Summary of Standards in Chapter 4.

3.1.12 If the accommodation is intended to house groups such as the elderly, physically disabled, or the mentally handicapped, then certain additional facilities may be necessary over and above the normal housing requirements (see 2.1.5). For instance, it is possible that the occupants will be dependent upon the provision of a degree of care (see 2.6.17). This may result in a need for extra rooms to be provided, partly for activities associated with the provision of care and partly to accommodate staff. Generally speaking, this will be most relevant in the context of hostels for special needs (see 3.5.32). However, some of the communal facilities are also encountered in sheltered housing and it is usual for sheltered housing schemes to include some one-person dwellings. Shared housing may also have an important role to play in catering

Bathrooms incorporating special types of equipment may be necessary in schemes catering for elderly or disabled people.

for the elderly or disabled, and purpose-designed dwellings intended for two or three elderly friends or siblings could occasionally be provided in sheltered housing schemes.

3.1.13 In schemes catering for special needs some enhancement of space standards may be appropriate. Each disabled person's private room should be increased in size by 3m^2 and the shared areas by about 10% principally in the bathrooms and circulation spaces likely to be used by those persons.

3.1.14 Parts of the building intended for occupation by elderly people or wheelchair users, will require a higher standard of heating than in general needs housing. Bed-sitting rooms, shared living spaces and bathrooms should be served by an installation capable of maintaining a temperature of 21°C when it is −1°C outside, and 15°C in the circulation areas.

3.1.15 Certain additional features such as specially designed bathroom fittings, grabrails, or warden call systems may also be necessary. Special design features and other requirements for elderly or disabled are covered in detail in Scottish Housing Handbook, Part 5: 'Housing for the Elderly' and Part 6: 'Housing for the Disabled'.

3.2 EXTERNAL WORKS

Site Layout

3.2.1 The form of buildings should be generally similar to other types of housing and an institutional appearance should be avoided. Most types of shared accommodation can be arranged in such a way as to resemble family dwellings in both internal layout and external appearance. In the case of hostels this may not be so easy to achieve: particular care needs to be taken over siting, massing and sensitive landscaping.

3.2.2 The introduction into an existing housing area of accommodation for single people, particularly shared dwellings, may arouse fears in residents of being disturbed by noise. Conversely, some single people may themselves fear noise disturbance from families with young children living nearby. Consideration should therefore be given to alleviating the possible effects of noise through the layout of buildings and external spaces at the design stage.

Recreation

3.2.3 A suitable choice of location would be near to parks or public open spaces, particularly if there was little space for private gardens or shared external areas associated with the housing itself. Where possible, it may be worthwhile using some external space for recreational purposes so long as this is kept away from buildings to avoid damage to windows or soft landscaping.

3.2.4 In large schemes, where it may be difficult to close off external spaces from public access routes, areas of soft landscaping and fencing may be subject to vandalism. Detailing of external works should be robust and any planting should be of hardy varieties. There are times when the presence of a caretaker on the site can be helpful in maintaining a casual surveillance over private and shared gardens. It is therefore desirable for his dwelling or office to be suitably located for this purpose.

Integration of hostels or shared accommodation into the community may be greatly assisted if the buildings present a domestic face to the world outside.

Design of the external spaces should allow for the likelihood of *ad hoc* recreational usage in schemes for young single people.

3.2.6 When designing vehicular access routes, it is important to ensure that adequate space is provided for refuse collection and for emergency services. In a street frontage scheme, the most straightforward solution is to use the existing roadway, or a bay off it, for these purposes. However, where the site is larger, a cul-de-sac off the main street may be required to gain access to some of the buildings. In this case proper turning areas will be required, to permit the vehicles to approach within an acceptable distance of the buildings.

3.2.7 Although it is obviously preferable for refuse collection to be made from individual dwellings, this may not be possible in large schemes. It may be necessary to incorporate some communal bin stores at suitable points. In multi-storey developments the use of refuse chutes and 'palladin' collectors might be considered. The local cleansing department should be consulted at an early stage to establish appropriate methods of refuse disposal.

Vehicular Access

3.2.5 In the design of external spaces in the development it is necessary to consider carefully vehicular access to the site. The design of vehicular access routes should be in accordance with the standards for housing generally and detailed information is contained in Scottish Housing Handbook, Part 3: 'Housing Development: Layout, Roads and Services'.

Car Parking and Garaging

3.2.8 It is necessary also to consider what level of car parking provision is appropriate or possible. In town centre sites, the scope for providing off-street parking spaces is often very limited. On the other hand, car ownership is unlikely to be so great for people in town centres as for those living in the suburbs or rural areas.

3.2.9 In general, car-ownership among single people is markedly less than for families (see Table 7).

TABLE 7

CAR OWNERSHIP IN ONE-PERSON PRIVATE HOUSEHOLDS

General Register Office for Scotland, Census 1981

Age		Total	No Car	1 Car	2 Cars	3+ Cars
Under Retirement	No.	129,282	82,926	43,495	2,288	573
	%	100	64.2	33.6	1.8	0.4
Over Retirement	No.	263,568	236,714	26,289	478	87
	%	100	89.8	10.0	0.2	—
All 1p Households	No.	392,850	319,640	69,784	2,766	660
	%	100	81.4	17.8	0.7	0.1
Other Households	No.	1,393,086	549,782	650,184	164,850	28,270
	%	100	39.5	46.7	11.8	2.0

Housing for Single People, Shared Accommodation and Hostels

The proportion of single person households who possess a motor car is less than one-third the equivalent proportion of other households. This is partly attributable to the large proportion of elderly single people who do not own a car. However, the level of car ownership among young single people is much higher and is actually comparable with the level for other households, although it is supposed that the proportion of car owners among the very young is somewhat smaller.

3.2.10 For the one-person and shared housing categories it should not be necessary to provide more than about one car space for every three residents, and rather less if the scheme is intended for occupation by the elderly.

3.2.11 In hostels, it is generally supposed that car ownership would be much lower than in the other categories. The parking provision would therefore be correspondingly smaller, with the possible exception of accommodation for migrant workers.

3.2.12 In all three categories, the number of car parking spaces provided at the outset should be kept to a minimum, although provision may be made to increase this if warranted by future demand.

3.2.13 In accommodation for young single persons, some provision should also be made for the parking of motorbikes and pedal cycles. The location of these parking spaces should take account of the need for security.

3.2.14 Although the need for garaging is generally expected to be very limited, in a large scheme it would be useful to provide a space for vehicle maintenance preferably under cover, or at least sheltered and screened off from other parts of the site.

Landscaping

3.2.15 In general, the nature of the space surrounding a development of housing for single people is likely to be conditioned strongly by the existing housing environment and it is essential that the materials and form of the landscaping are appropriate to that situation. Where there are heavily trafficked pedestrian routes, these should be adequately paved. Any adjacent soft landscaping should be carefully selected to ensure its survival in a harsh environment.

3.2.16 In semi-private zones shared by the occupants, greater use of soft landscaping should be possible. However, young single people are unlikely to wish to have their own gardens and it would be preferable for any shared open space to be com-

munally maintained. This may be organised by the housing authority who would levy a charge included in the rent. Other arrangements might include contract gardening and possibly sharing some of the tasks between occupants on a rota basis. Alternatively, this work could be included as part of the caretaker's duties.

3.2.17 Single people are likely to appreciate somewhere sheltered from the wind to sit out in the sun on a summer's day. A shared garden with terraces close to the buildings and grassed areas protected by walls, trees and shrubs would undoubtedly be valued and it should be reasonably easy to maintain once planting has become established.

Space for parking or storage of bicycles may be needed in some schemes.

Pedestrian routes should be designed to minimise wear and tear on soft landscaping.

3.2.18 It is desirable for some part of the external space to be used as a communal drying green and it would be appropriate for this to be associated with the laundry in large schemes.

Private Open Spaces

3.2.19 In small schemes consisting of one-person dwellings intended for those who had become more settled in life, or for the elderly, small private gardens would be desirable and would enable each occupant to be provided with an external drying area. However, the advantages of providing a limited amount of private external space for dwellings entered from ground level should not encourage the provision of balconies for flats in multi-storey schemes. Balconies have generally not been successful in the past. Their use for sitting out or clothes drying is obviously much affected by the vagaries of the Scottish climate and the awkward constructional details which arise in their design have frequently led to water penetration, or heat loss and condensation.

3.2.20 More detailed information concerning the choice of suitable building forms, design of external spaces, and details of landscaping and planting is included in Scottish Housing Handbook, Part 3: 'Housing Development: Layout, Roads and Services'.

3.3 DETAIL DESIGN OF ONE-PERSON HOUSING

3.3.1 The design of one-person dwellings should in every respect be in accordance with the standards for general needs housing and should fulfil all the requirements of the Building Regulations for buildings in occupancy sub-groups A1 or A2. There are two dwelling types to be considered: one-apartment dwellings and two-apartment dwellings (see 2.5.4–2.5.8).

One-Apartment Dwellings

3.3.2 In one-person dwellings the basic unit is clearly different from the other types of shared accommodation in that the entire unit is for the exclusive use of an individual. In the past, the minimum space standards for mainstream housing have included an area for one-person dwellings based on the assumption that this would normally be a large bed-sitting room with associated kitchen, bathroom, storage and circulation space. This is the smallest type of independent dwelling suitable for a single person. In one-apartment dwellings, the gross floor area should be not less than $32.5m^2$ for flats or $33.0m^2$ for houses.

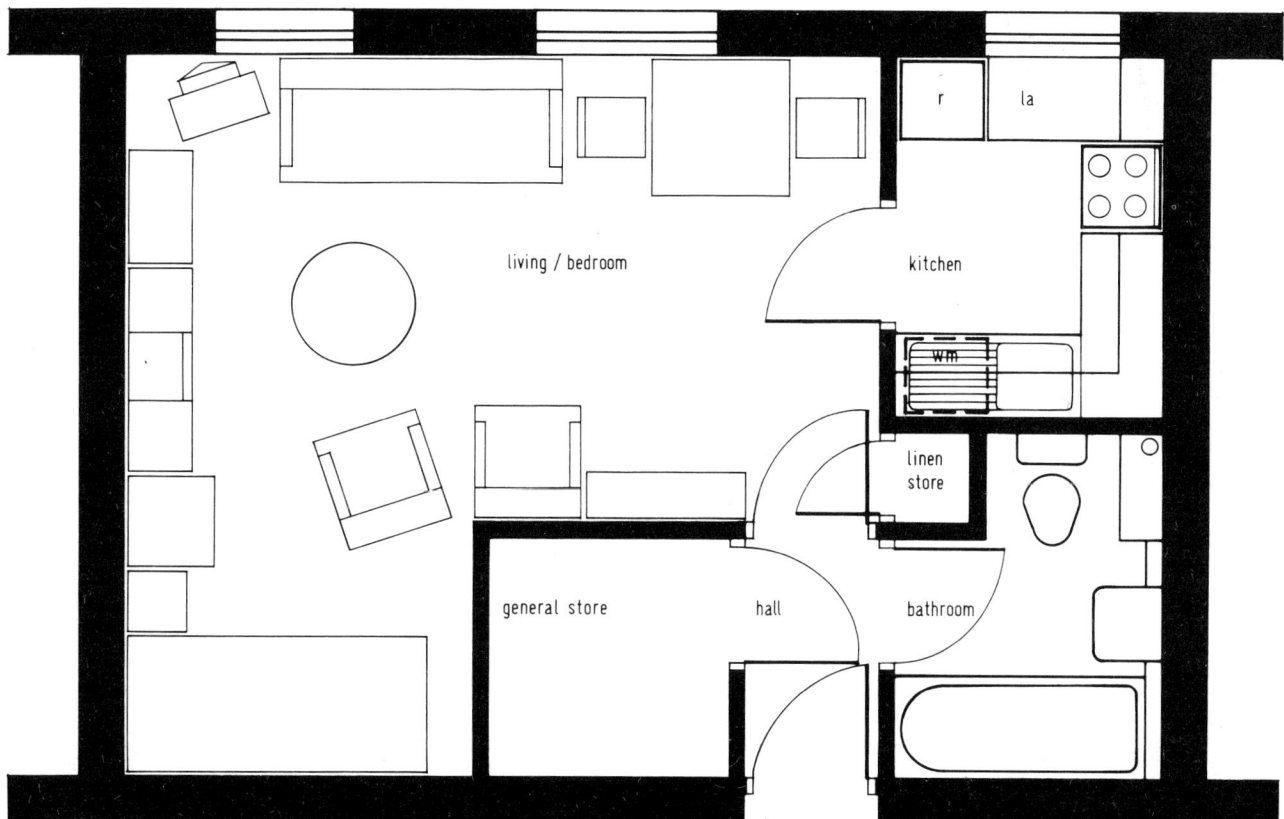

one person / one apartment dwelling (6900 × 4800 = 33·12m²)   1:50

Housing for Single People, Shared Accommodation and Hostels

one person / two apartment dwelling (5900×6300 = 37.17 m²)   1:50

Two-Apartment Dwellings

3.3.3 In two-apartment dwellings the living room and single bedroom are separate and this will require rather more floor area than for one-apartment dwellings. In recent years a considerable amount of interest has been shown in two-apartment dwellings especially among housing associations providing sheltered housing for the elderly or other special needs groups. Such associations have found that the standard bedsitter flat has sometimes been not big enough to accommodate tenants' furniture and this has led to requests for dwellings with a separate bedroom. In two-apartment dwellings the gross floor area should not be less than 37m².

Other Spaces within each Dwelling

3.3.4 In addition to the living and sleeping areas the gross floor areas include a dining area, kitchen, bathroom, general storage, linen store, internal circulation and partitions.

3.3.5 The dining area can be either part of the kitchen or part of the living room.

3.3.6 In flatted schemes up to 1.5m² of the general storage space for each dwelling can be an external store at ground level. Separate spaces are required for storage of refuse, and possibly for fuel where necessary for the type of heating appliances used.

Optional Facilities

3.3.7 There are various optional features or communal facilities some of which may be desirable in schemes containing one-person dwellings. Many of these features would not normally be included in small schemes, but they might be appropriate in large flatted developments. For example, if a housing development for single people is provided in an area which lacks community facilities it would be desirable to include certain items for communal use.

Laundry

3.3.8 Perhaps the most obvious and useful communal facility would be a laundry. This should be equipped with sinks and commercial standard washing machines and tumbler-dryers. One of each item could suffice for up to 30 tenants; for a greater number two or more of each may be necessary. It should also contain worktops, storage units and space for ironing. Even if tenants possess their own washing machines, a tumbler-dryer would be useful as drying clothes may be difficult in the confined space of a flat.

Shop

3.3.9 Where there are no shops nearby, or where they do not remain open at weekends or in the evenings, consideration should be given to including a small general store, which should be conveniently located for residents of the neighbourhood (see 3.3.16).

Common Room

3.3.10 It is desirable for large schemes of predominantly single person dwellings or shared flats, to be provided with some communal lounge space. This need not be more than 0.5m² per person with 20m² being the minimum room area.

3.3.11 Many single people, especially the young, can experience initial loneliness when they move to a new area for employment or take the first steps towards independence by setting up home. They are probably more likely to look to the housing scheme for new friends and the provision of a lounge area close to the main entrance would encourage people to meet on a casual basis, as well as providing an area suitable for holding meetings or parties. In smaller schemes or in situations where there is a substantial proportion of older single people, it is

Casual lounge area close to main entrance.

doubtful if common rooms and associated spaces would be used to any great extent. In these circumstances they could well be omitted.

3.3.12 Associated with a common room there should be cloakroom and WCs, and possibly a small tea-bar or pantry. Nearby would be a public telephone and notice boards.

Common Access, Lifts and Plant

3.3.13 In schemes comprising one-person dwellings, shared dwellings, or a combination of both, these may be either houses each entered from ground level, or low-rise or medium-rise flats entered off a common access stair. However, in large developments the dwellings might be provided in blocks of flats with extensive communal entrances and circulation areas. A cleaner's store with sink, worktop and shelves may be provided in connection with communal circulation areas.

3.3.14 A plant room and electrical switch room may be required in large flatted developments, and a lift must be provided when the building exceeds 4 storeys in height.

Maintenance, Deliveries and Security

3.3.15 Maintenance of the communal areas will require a particular housing management input and in a large scheme this might involve the provision of a caretaker. A 3–5 person mainstream dwelling and a small office could be provided for this purpose. The services of a caretaker would overcome the difficulties commonly experienced by single people at work, like making arrangements for deliveries or maintenance repairs. A resident caretaker might also be responsible for cleaning services, maintaining heating systems and boiler rooms, organising fuel supply, meter-readings and collecting rent.

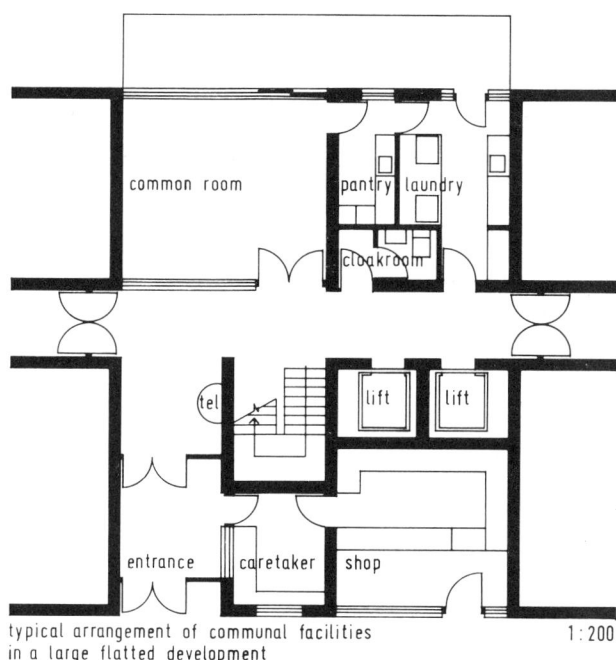

common room   pantry laundry

cloakroom

tel   lift   lift

entrance   caretaker   shop

typical arrangement of communal facilities   1:200
in a large flatted development

Housing for Single People, Shared Accommodation and Hostels

Entry-phone system in the main entrance lobby to a multi-storey building.

3.3.16 The presence of a caretaker can also be advantageous for security and it is preferable for his dwelling and office to be sited to permit casual surveillance of access routes into the scheme rather than rigid control of the main entrance door. Provision of a caretaker service could be associated with the running of a small shop.

3.3.17 Single residents in a flatted development should be encouraged to regard dwellings as independent units. For instance, it is preferable for postal and other regular deliveries to be made to each front door rather than to lockers or pigeon-holes at the main entrance. Apart from the inconvenience for tenants having to collect articles from lockers, there is also the problem of security in such a system and this might place an unreasonable responsibility upon the caretaker.

3.3.18 Except in cases where dwellings can be entered from ground level, it is desirable for an entry-phone system to be installed so that the main entrance door can be kept locked at all times. This is particularly important if there are communal facilities near to the entrance as they would be prone to vandalism if left open to the public.

Casual surveillance of the main entrance from nearby windows.

3.4 DETAIL DESIGN OF SHARED HOUSING

3.4.1 The design of shared dwellings will be similar to the design of mainstream dwellings. The dwellings will fulfil all the requirements of the Building Regulations for buildings in occupancy sub-groups A1 or A2. The size of households will range from 2–8 single persons (4–6 being preferred). There are two ways of providing this accommodation: by building purpose-designed dwellings or by using existing mainstream dwellings (see 2.5.9.–2.5.13).

Purpose-Designed Shared Dwellings

3.4.2 Shared housing can be provided in purpose-designed dwellings with a gross floor area per person not less than that shown in Table 5 (see 3.1.4–3.1.10).

Using Mainstream Dwellings

3.4.3 Alternatively shared housing may be provided by simply using mainstream housing in such a way that in each dwelling the total number of apartments is at least one greater than the number of single people expected to occupy that dwelling. Thus, there would be a bedroom for each person.

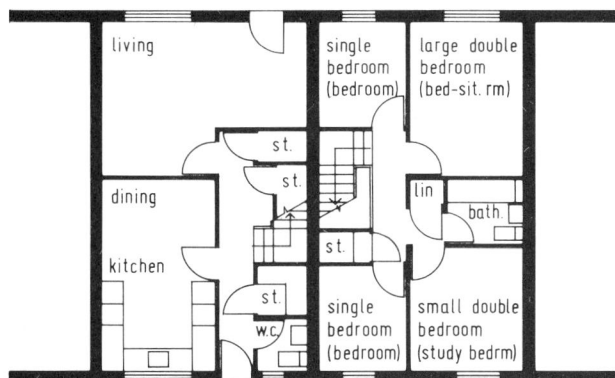

Shared dwellings: purpose-designed flatted accommodation.

The living room and the remainder of the dwelling would be shared between the occupants (see 3.6.1).

3.4.4 It would obviously be desirable for such dwellings to meet the same standards as purpose-designed shared housing, and some modifications may be required in order to achieve this aim. However, a realistic and flexible attitude should be adopted in deciding how much modification is

example of 6 person mainstream dwelling
suitable for sharing by 4 single people   1 : 200

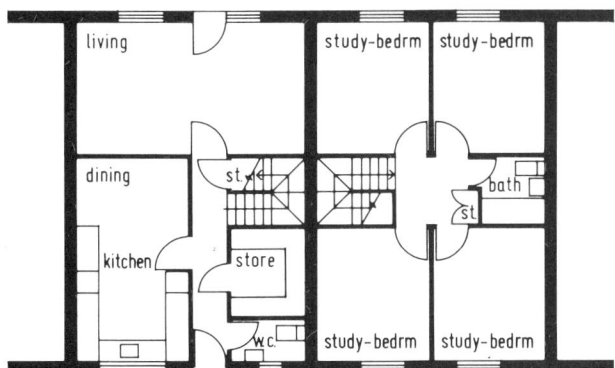

similar house type, purpose-designed as
a shared dwelling for 4 persons   1 : 200

Shared dwellings: existing mainstream dwellings used by groups of single people.

Housing for Single People, Shared Accommodation and Hostels

reasonable or practicable in the particular circumstances. It is therefore left to the discretion of the providers of housing to determine how best to allocate the available financial resources (see 3.6.8).

Private Space

3.4.5 There are three different types and sizes of private accommodation. These correspond in size to the three types of bedroom commonly encountered in mainstream housing: single bedrooms; small double bedrooms (designed for a double bed); and large double bedrooms (capable of accommodating two single beds). The equivalent rooms for single people are bedrooms ($7m^2$ minimum), study-bedrooms ($10m^2$ minimum), and bed-sitting rooms ($13m^2$ minimum). The distinctions between these in size and the furniture which each may be expected to contain, are shown in the diagrams.

3.4.6 It would be normal to use study-bedrooms for shared housing, and bed-sitting rooms for hostels. However, within the recommended gross floor areas per person, shown in Tables 5 and 6, there would be scope for varying the balance between private and shared spaces, by using a different type of private room and reducing or increasing the size of shared living space in compensation. For instance, a shared dwelling might be designed with bed-sitting rooms in place of the slightly smaller study-bedrooms; in which case it would be appropriate to reduce the shared living space. Or a hostel could be proposed with study-bedrooms in place of bed-sitting rooms, when it would be possible to provide rather larger communal areas.

3.4.7 It may occasionally be desirable to provide a small number of double rooms in purpose-designed shared housing or hostels, and examples of a double study-bedroom ($16m^2$ minimum) and a double bed-sitting room ($19m^2$ minimum) are also shown in the diagrams.

The private room for each occupant will generally be functioning to some extent as a living room as well as a bedroom.

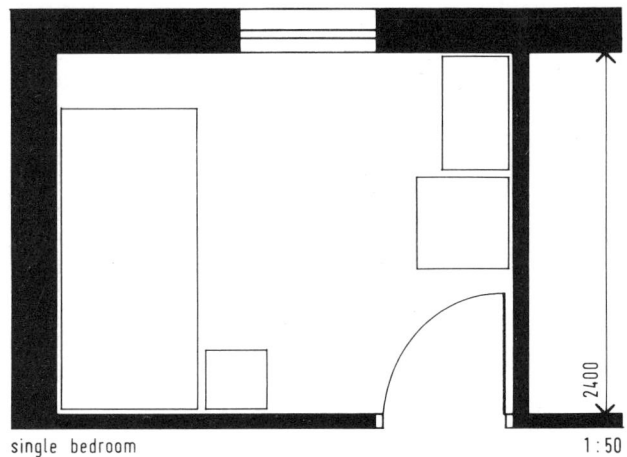

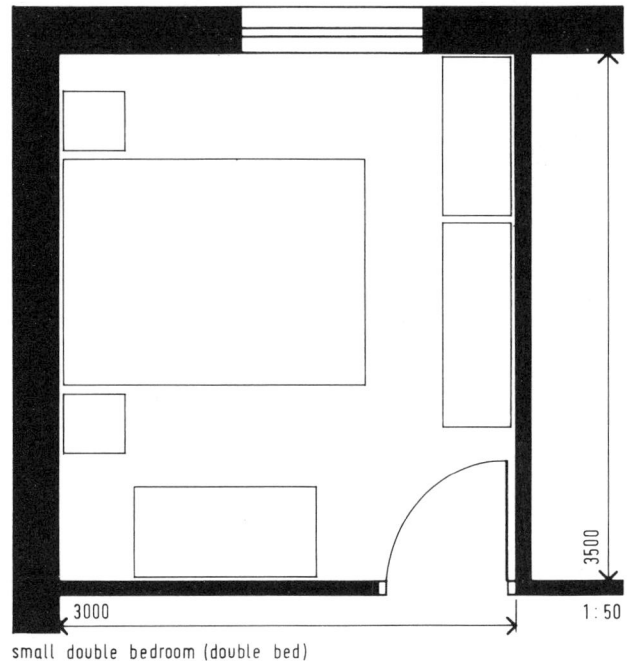

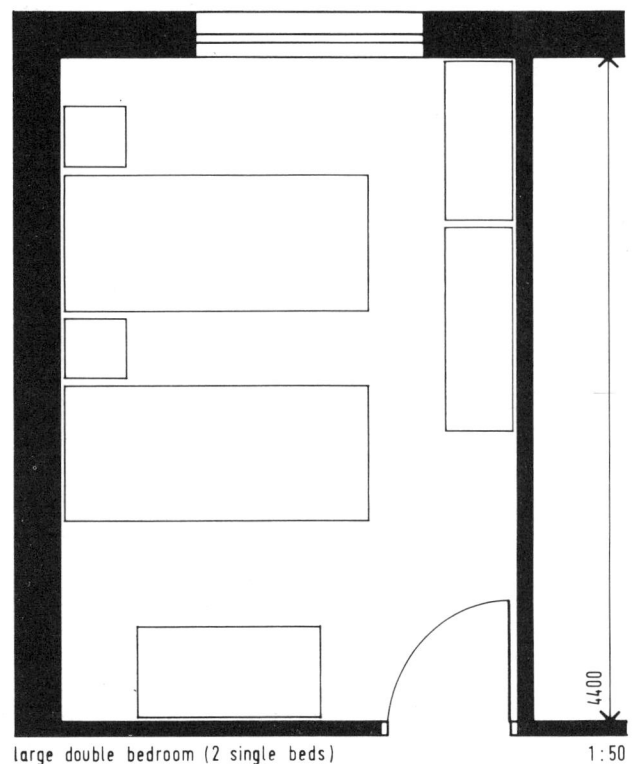

single bedroom   1:50

small double bedroom (double bed)   1:50

large double bedroom (2 single beds)   1:50

It may occasionally be appropriate to include a few double rooms.

More space in a double room, for additional furniture.

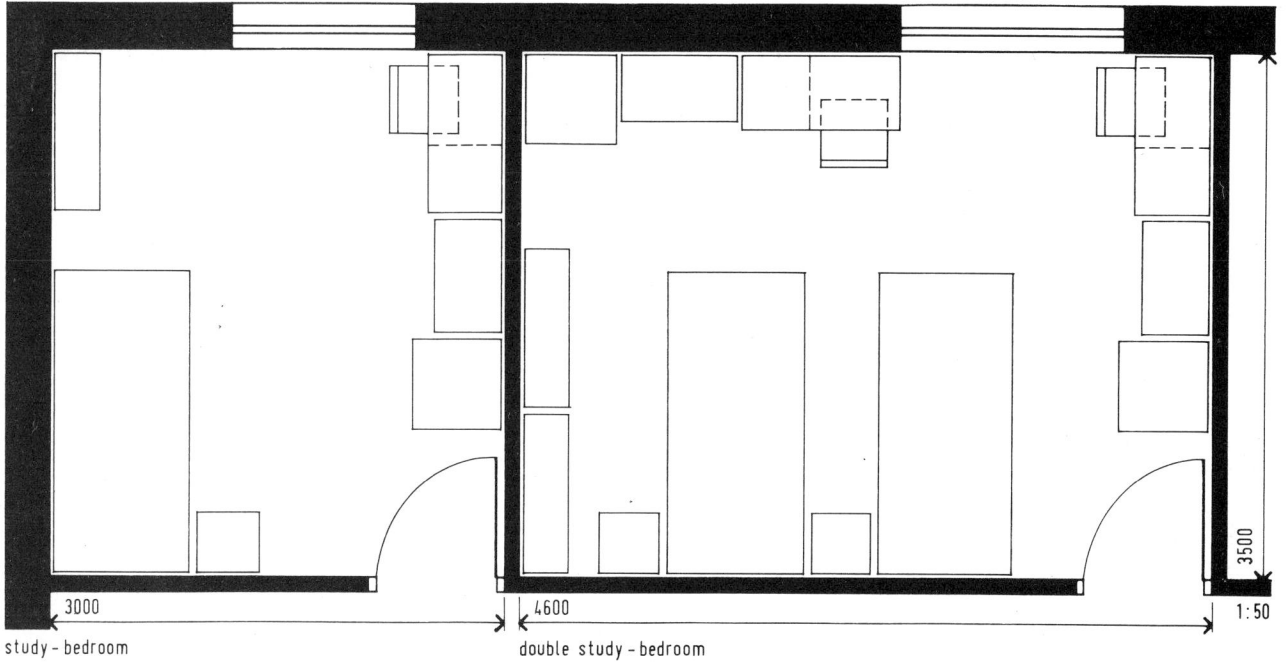

3000

study – bedroom

4600

double study – bedroom

3500

1:50

bed – sitting room

double bed – sitting room

4400

1:50

Housing for Single People, Shared Accommodation and Hostels

Furnishings

3.4.8 A typical scheme of shared housing for single people could contain a mixture of furnished and unfurnished accommodation: some dwellings could be partly furnished or equipped with loose furnishings only. Although it would be normal for hostels to be furnished, there are certain types of schemes for elderly people where comparatively large unfurnished bed-sitting rooms are provided with the specific intention of permitting residents to bring furniture with them from their previous homes (see 3.5.33). Some housing associations have already been active in the provision of this form of accommodation.

3.4.9 Within each private space, built-in or fitted storage units can be economical in use of space, although they naturally result in some loss of flexibility in the way the room can be arranged. Fitted furniture could include a wardrobe, chest of drawers, open shelves, desk with a pin-board above, and in the case of bed-sitting rooms in a hostel, a wash basin set into a worktop with a mirror fixed above and a towel-rail. Loose furniture such as a bed, bed-side cabinet, chair, curtains, bedspread and rug could be hired or rented from the landlord as and when required.

3.4.10 Wardrobes should always be provided with locks. In hostels, the doors to bed-sitting rooms should also be lockable.

Wardrobe and vanitory unit, built in to a single bed-sit.

Residents may wish to bring items of furniture with them from previous homes.

Loose furniture provided by the building owner.

Built-in storage fitment with lockable door.

Shared Space

3.4.11 The shared space includes living room, dining area, kitchen, bathroom and WC, general storage, linen store, internal circulation and partitions.

Living and Dining Areas

3.4.12 The main shared living area is unlikely to differ significantly from the living room in a normal mainstream dwelling. It is preferable for at least part of this to be provided as a room separate from the dining room and kitchen. In dwellings for up to 5

Living/dining room in a shared dwelling with the kitchen off one end.

persons the dining and kitchen areas may well be combined. In larger dwellings the dining area and kitchen would normally be in adjoining but separate spaces.

3.4.13 An alternative to both separate and combined dining/kitchen areas is the large farmhouse kitchen. This includes some sitting space as well as the dining area, with the working kitchen at one end of the room or divided off by peninsular storage units or a breakfast bar. This type of arrangement might be appropriate where the dwelling was sufficiently large to warrant the inclusion of an additional living room separated from this space, or where a larger private room was provided for each resident with a correspondingly smaller amount of space available for the shared living areas (see 3.4.6).

Dining/kitchen in a shared dwelling with a separate living room.

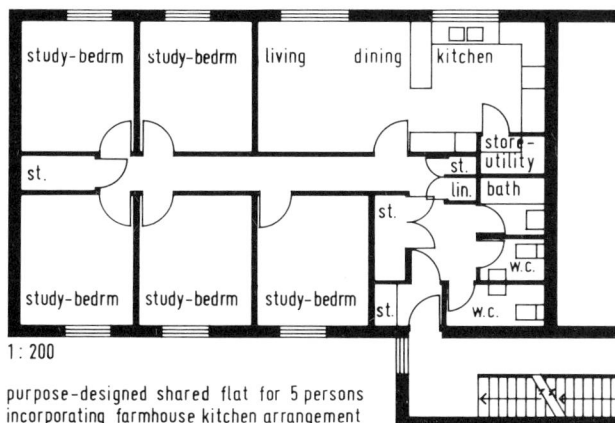

1 : 200

purpose-designed shared flat for 5 persons incorporating farmhouse kitchen arrangement

Housing for Single People, Shared Accommodation and Hostels

3.4.14 The occupants of shared dwellings will sometimes have meals together, perhaps taking turns to do the cooking and other household chores. However, in many cases they may act independently and take most of their meals alone. Thus, in larger dwellings it would be necessary to allow rather more kitchen storage accommodation than normal in a general needs house. A double base-unit for each person together with a communal ventilated larder unit and shelving or high level units for communal storage should be sufficient. In larger dwellings it would also be desirable to provide a double sink and drainer for the accumulation of dirty dishes, spaces for a full height fridge/freezer cabinet, extra cooker or separate hob and oven units and possibly a dishwasher. This would be in addition to the spaces normally allowed for kitchen equipment in mainstream housing.

3.4.15 For larger shared dwellings, especially in schemes not having a laundry, it would be desirable to provide a small utility room off the kitchen for clothes washing and drying equipment. This space could also be used to accommodate a heating boiler and broom cupboard. In this way the more noisy and untidy activities can be kept away from the kitchen and communal living areas. This would be particularly important if a 'farmhouse kitchen' arrangement was used.

Larger or additional items of equipment may be required in large shared dwellings.

A separate utility room is desirable in larger dwellings, particularly if a dining/kitchen or farmhouse kitchen arrangement is used.

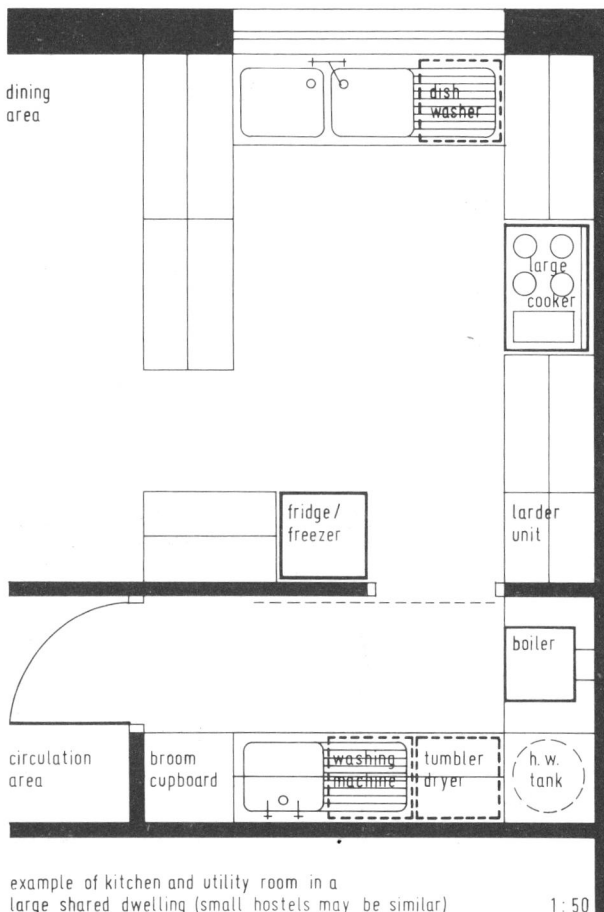

example of kitchen and utility room in a
large shared dwelling (small hostels may be similar)   1:50

Bathrooms, WCs and Wash-Hand Basins

3.4.16 The design of the sanitary accommodation in existing mainstream dwellings used for sharing would conform with the normal standards for general needs housing. The number of fittings per person would, of course, be increased somewhat by the fact that the dwellings were under-occupied in relation to the number of bedspaces in mainstream family housing (see 3.4.2, 3.6.1). In purpose-designed shared dwellings for four or more single persons, a second WC fitting should be provided, and for six or more persons a second bath or shower fitting. The bath-shower and WC fittings should preferably be arranged in separate compartments with a wash-hand basin in each.

3.4.17 It would not normally be necessary to provide wash-hand basins in each study-bedroom. If they were so provided, it would be reasonable to combine the bathrooms and WCs into a smaller number of compartments. The various possible arrangements of sanitary fittings are shown in Table 8.

General and Linen Storage

3.4.18 As residents are likely to be independent they will probably need rather more space for general storage. A volume of 3m³ per person is suggested as a minimum and this should preferably be arranged in several shallow cupboards well-supplied with shelving, rather than all being combined into a few large deep cupboards where stored articles are not so readily accessible or identifiable. It may be possible to include this as part of each study-bedroom or alongside it, although it would be useful to have some of the storage space in the form of shared cupboards. In flatted developments it is desirable to have a small amount of the storage space at ground level for each dwelling. A linen cupboard should be provided additional to and separate from the general storage.

TABLE 8

PROVISION OF SANITARY FITTINGS IN SHARED HOUSING

B/S—Bath or Shower; WC—Water Closet Fitting; WHB—Wash Hand Basin

No. of Persons	1	2	3	4	5	6	7	8
Arrangement of fittings in Shared Housing *without WHBs* in each study-bedroom	B/S WC WHB	B/S WC WHB	B/S WHB	B/S WC WHB	B/S WHB	B/S WHB	B/S WHB	B/S WHB
			WC WHB	WC WHB	WC WHB	B/S WC WHB	B/S WHB	B/S WHB
					WC WHB	WC WHB	WC WHB	WC WHB
							WC WHB	WC WHB
Arrangement of fittings in Shared Housing *with WHBs* in each study-bedroom	B/S WC WHB	B/S WC WHB	B/S WC WHB	B/S WC WHB	B/S WC WHB	B/S WC WHB	B/S WC WHB	B/S WC WHB
			WC WHB	WC WHB	WC WHB	B/S WC WHB	B/S WC WHB	B/S WC WHB

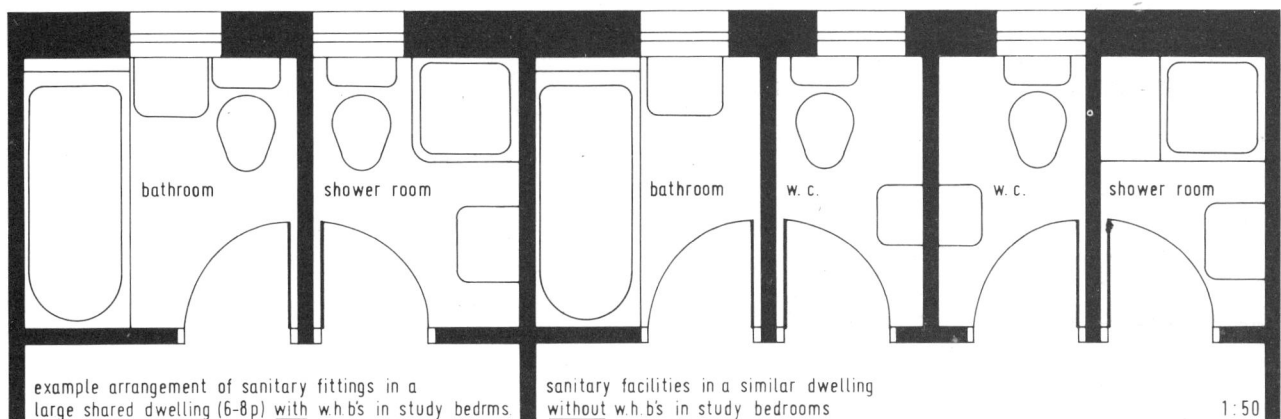

example arrangement of sanitary fittings in a large shared dwelling (6-8p) <u>with</u> w.h.b's in study bedrms.

sanitary facilities in a similar dwelling <u>without</u> w.h.b's in study bedrooms

1:50

Housing for Single People, Shared Accommodation and Hostels

Sound Attenuation

3.4.19 Noise transmission between rooms can be a serious nuisance and a major source of friction between residents. This is particularly important for some client groups, such as nurses, who may work shifts or keep irregular hours. It is therefore essential that Grade 1 standards of insulation for airborne and impact sound transmission are achieved. This applies not only to the party walls and floors dividing dwellings in a grouped development from one another, but also to the partitions and floors between individual private rooms in shared housing and hostels. This may be difficult to achieve in partitions separating private rooms from access corridors or other circulation spaces because of doors. Sound reduction between rooms may be helped by avoiding the location of doors immediately opposite one another across a passage.

3.4.20 Doors to individual occupants' rooms should be of solid core construction for purposes of sound insulation, and draught stripping of the edges could be considered for the same reason.

3.4.21 Airborne sound from open windows may also create a problem of noise, and care should be taken over the disposition of windows to avoid placing them in close proximity to one another and especially not immediately opposite nearby dwellings. Outward opening sashes can aggravate sound transmission between windows in the same elevation of a building, and if possible these types should be avoided.

Heating Appliances

3.4.22 Individual residents' rooms in shared housing and hostels should be heated to the same level as living rooms in mainstream dwellings. In other respects, the standards of heating and thermal insulation should be equivalent to mainstream housing. Care should be taken over the choice and location of radiators or other heating appliances to minimise their intrusion into usable space within rooms and to avoid interruption of wall surfaces against which residents will place furniture. Heating appliances should be controllable within each resident's room.

Power Points

3.4.23 The provision of electrical socket outlets should generally be in accordance with the standards for mainstream housing. However, in purpose designed accommodation it would be appropriate to increase the number of points to cater for additional equipment likely to be used in residents' rooms intended partly to provide living space for individual occupants. It is therefore suggested that study-bedrooms, and bed-sitting rooms should have at least two double socket outlets at low level and an additional double socket above the fitted desk top. In double rooms an extra double socket should be provided at low level.

3.4.24 In some hostels the power points in each resident's room are controlled by a prepayment meter, but in many cases there is no separate metering. In shared housing a single standard meter for the whole dwelling is sufficient.

Window Cleaning

3.4.25 It may sometimes be difficult to arrange access for window cleaners during the day when residents are out at work. It may therefore be necessary for residents to clean the windows themselves, and the choice of window design should take this into account.

Telephones

3.4.26 In shared accommodation for single people it would not be normal for telephones to be provided in resident's rooms. A telephone should be installed in the hall or communal living area. To avoid problems over sharing telephone bills, it would be preferable to install a pay telephone rather than the normal domestic instrument.

Optional Facilities

3.4.27 The range of possible additional features mentioned in the context of one-person housing, eg laundry, shop, common room and caretaker's office (see 3.3.7–3.3.18) might also be considered desirable in some shared housing developments.

3.5 DETAIL DESIGN OF HOSTELS

3.5.1 Hostels differ from mainstream housing in that they cater for a larger number of occupants than would normally be encountered in a dwelling and they generally provide some communal services. It is likely that the number of occupants will be rarely less than 10 and it may be as many as 50 or more. The design of the accommodation will be in accordance with the standards prescribed in the Building Regulations for buildings in occupancy sub-group A3, although certain types of residential homes for special needs may be classified A4. There are two types of hostel to be considered: staffed hostels and self-catering hostels (see 2.5.14–2.5.18).

Staffed Hostels

3.5.2 It is usual for hostels to be staffed, and to be designed on the assumption that all residents will be given a full catering service or at least one main meal each day. The gross floor area per person should be not less than that shown in Table 6 (see 3.1.4–3.1.10).

Self-Catering Hostels

3.5.3 Hostels may occasionally be designed as self-catering accommodation where no meals are provided for residents and where staff are limited to wardens, possibly on a part-time basis only.

3.5.4 The accommodation would be similar to staffed hostels except that the pantries for each group of bed-sitting rooms would be replaced by a domestic kitchen with space for dining. The communal living areas would be reduced in size, and the main kitchen with associated storage spaces and staff rooms would be omitted entirely (see 3.5.10, 3.5.22).

Detail Design of the Private Spaces

3.5.5. The basic unit of private accommodation in hostels will be similar to that which is described in the context of shared housing (see 3.4.5–3.4.10, 3.4.19–3.4.25).

Shared Spaces

3.5.6 The shared space includes communal living areas, warden's office, bathrooms, WCs, kitchen, larder, bulk store, cold store, pantries, laundry room, cleaner's stores, linen stores, general storage, external storage, plant rooms, entrance hall, corridors, ducts, partitions and staircases.

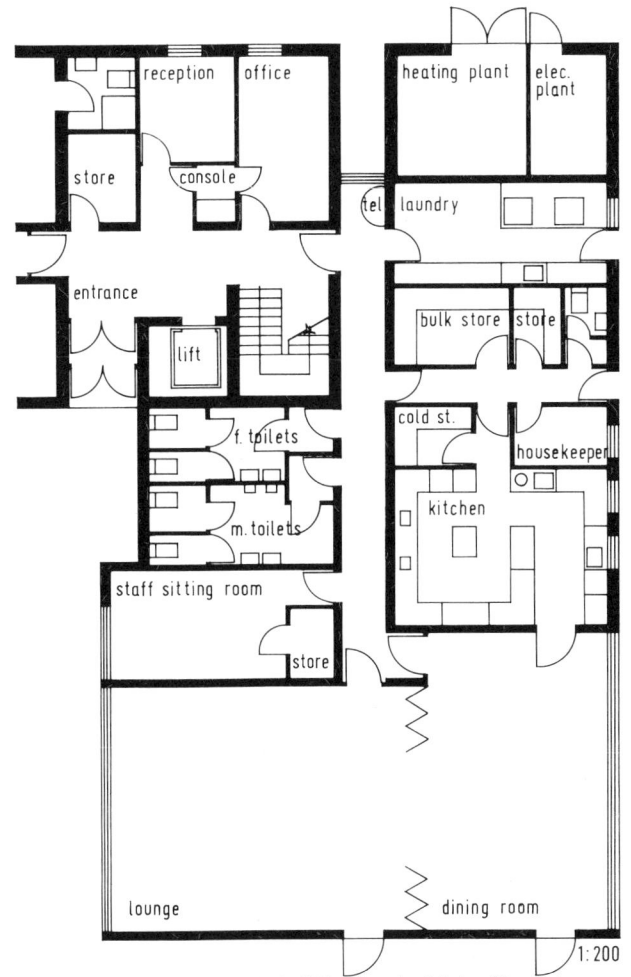

typical example of communal facilities in a hostel for 30 people

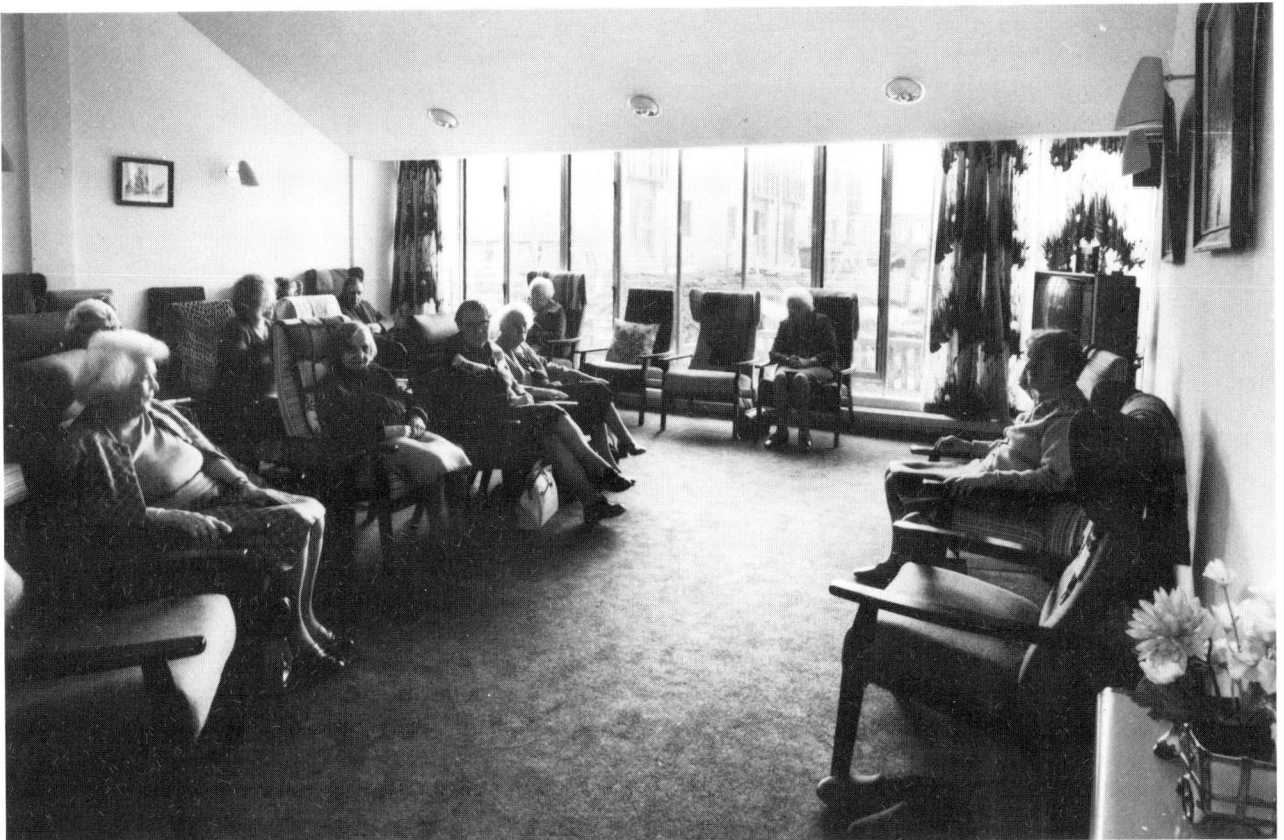

The communal sitting room in a hostel should present a comfortable and welcoming appearance.

Housing for Single People, Shared Accommodation and Hostels

Communal dining room, with a pleasant view to the outside.

Sitting room adjacent to the dining room in a small hostel.

Dining room separated from the kitchen by means of a worktop or tea-bar.

Living and Dining Areas

3.5.7 It is important that these areas are of comfortable and welcoming appearance. Preferably they should be near entrance or internal circulation routes so that residents are encouraged to regard them as the focus of social activities. Residents should not feel obliged to confine themselves to their own bed-sitting rooms because of unsuitable living areas.

3.5.8 The living area should not be like a public waiting room. Some cosy corners could be provided by subdividing the space or by careful arrangement of furniture. The communal living areas should also be arranged so that different activities can take place in different parts of the space. In particular, if it is decided to include a communal TV, then it would be desirable to put this in an alcove away from the general sitting area, or better still in a separate room.

3.5.9 In staffed hostels, the dining area should preferably be separate from the kitchen but possibly linked to it by means of a hatch, a pantry or a tea-bar. The living area could open directly off the dining room or be part of the same space perhaps with some form of visual separation such as shelving or fixed seating.

3.5.10 In self-catering hostels the space allowed for dining should be divided up so as to provide a meals area associated with the kitchen beside each group of bed-sitting rooms (3.5.4). It would be desirable to have a tea-bar serving the communal living areas, particularly if there is no kitchen nearby.

Cloakrooms

3.5.11 Separate male and female cloakrooms and WCs should always be provided near entrance halls and communal living areas. Cloakrooms should be suitably located for use by staff, especially if there are no separate staff WCs elsewhere.

Access for Disabled

3.5.12 The main entrance hall, the communal living areas and any cloakrooms or WCs associated with the 'public' areas, should always be designed for convenient access by disabled people.

Warden's Office and Reception Room

3.5.13 Most hostels will be supervised by a warden and he/she should be provided with an office, preferably situated close to the main entrance and communal living areas. Location of an office near to the entrance permits casual surveillance of people entering or leaving the building. This is particularly important if residents are out during the day, and it also has the advantage of providing a contact point for maintenance services and day-time deliveries. As well as administering the hostel, the warden occasionally has to discuss matters in private with residents or visitors and an office is needed on such occasions.

3.5.14 Office equipment should include a desk with drawers or a filing cabinet beneath, and shelving or possibly a full-height shelved cupboard to one side. A small glazed hatch to the entrance hall would be a useful feature and this could be located above the fitted desk top, with a pin-board and possibly an adjustable desk lamp mounted on the wall beside the hatch. There should be sufficient space in the remainder of the room to provide at least two easy chairs in addition to an upright chair at the desk. It is important for the door, hatch and storage units to be securely lockable to safeguard documents and cash. Space could be provided for a small safe if there was any possibility of significant amounts of cash being kept on the premises.

3.5.15 If the hostel is intended for elderly or severely handicapped people, a warden call system, linked to a control console in the warden's office, would be installed. Warden call systems are described in Scottish Housing Handbook, Part 5: 'Housing for the Elderly'.

3.5.16 In large schemes, it may be desirable to have a separate reception room beside the warden's office. In this case the office could be reduced in area

to accommodate the administrative and supervisory functions alone. The reception room should be decorated and furnished as a small domestic sitting room.

Telephones

3.5.17 A public telephone cubicle should always be provided in the entrance hall and in large hostels it may be necessary to have more than one. A separate telephone line should be provided for the warden's office and possibly the housekeeper's office. It would be worthwhile for house telephones on each floor of a large hostel to be linked to the warden's or housekeeper's offices.

Public telephone in the entrance hall.

The warden's office.

Warden's office with reception room opening directly off the main entrance hall.

Some people find it easier to use a shower rather than a bath and it is desirable to include some of each type of fitting.

Bathrooms, WCs and Wash-Hand Basins

3.5.18 In hostels the normal provision should be one bath or shower, and one WC (with wash-hand basin), to every five residents. As wash-hand basins will normally be provided in each bed-sitting room, it would not be necessary to have a basin in the bathroom unless a WC fitting was included. The various possible arrangements of sanitary fittings are illustrated in Table 9.

3.5.19 In a large scheme where, for instance, one floor could accommodate ten to fifteen people, it may be possible to group all the sanitary accommodation within easy reach of all residents' rooms. This would obviously reduce installation costs. Moreover, it would enable showers to be provided as well as baths and so give residents a choice of facilities. In general, it is thought that the majority of people prefer baths, but it is clearly beneficial if a number of showers can be provided particularly if residents are manual workers. Showers would then

TABLE 9

PROVISION OF SANITARY FITTINGS IN HOSTELS

B/S—Bath or Shower; WC—Water Closet Fitting; WHB—Wash-Hand Basin

No. of Persons in each group	3	4	5	6	7	8	9	10	Etc
Arrangement of fittings in Hostels, for each group of bed-sitting rooms, *with WHBs* in each bed-sit	B/S WC WHB	B/S	B/S	As 3+3	As 3+4	As 4+4	As 4+5	As 5+5	Etc
		WC WHB	WC WHB						

Plus at least one WC+WHB off the entrance hall (Pref sep M+F).
Additional sanitary fittings may be required in the staff areas in a larger hostel.

If WHBs are not provided in each bed-sit, an additional WHB should be included in the compartment containing the B/S on its own.

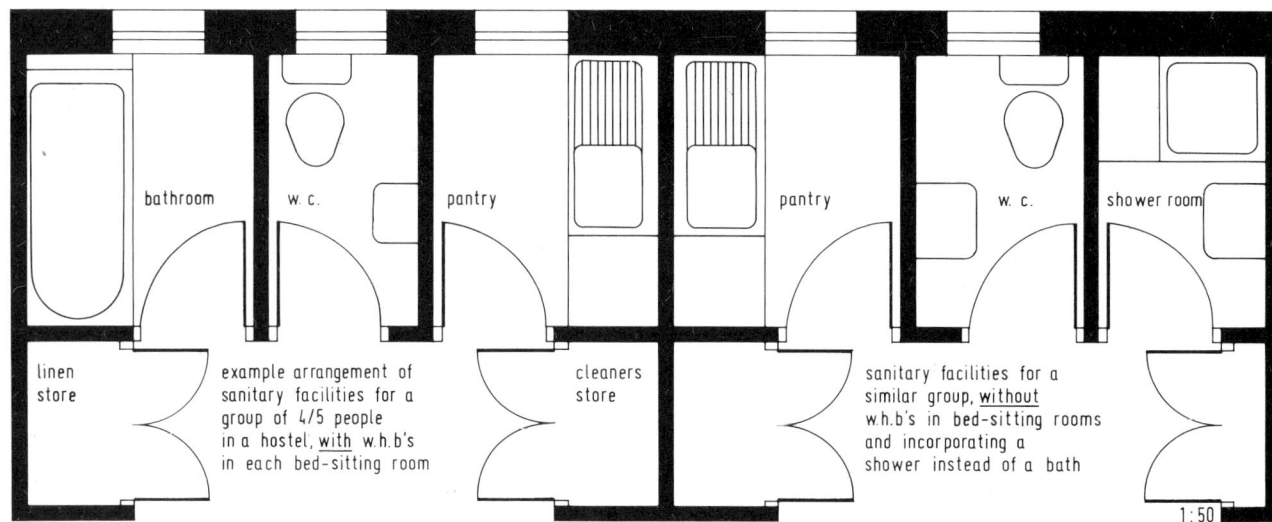

linen store

bathroom   w. c.   pantry

example arrangement of sanitary facilities for a group of 4/5 people in a hostel, with w.h.b's in each bed-sitting room

cleaners store

pantry   w. c.   shower room

sanitary facilities for a similar group, without w.h.b's in bed-sitting rooms and incorporating a shower instead of a bath

1:50

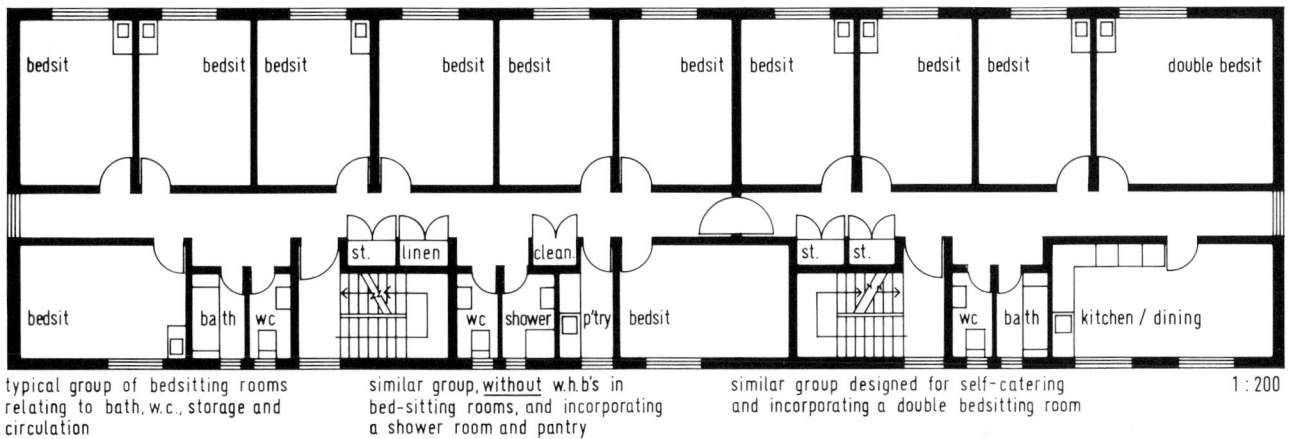

typical group of bedsitting rooms relating to bath, w.c., storage and circulation

similar group, <u>without</u> w.h.b's in bed-sitting rooms, and incorporating a shower room and pantry

similar group designed for self-catering and incorporating a double bedsitting room

1:200

be preferable both for their economy in the use of hot water and for the relatively short time taken to wash compared with baths. In large hostels grouping together of sanitary facilities has the additional advantage of permitting the WCs to be in separate male and female sections.

Kitchens

3.5.20 In staffed hostels, the main kitchen should normally be designed so that sufficient meals can be prepared to cope with maximum possible demand ie all residents having a meal at the same time. In very small hostels, a kitchen of domestic scale will be adequate. However, in larger hostels the kitchen will have to accommodate all the items needed for full-scale catering with separate zones for food preparation, serving and washing-up, and a comprehensive range of kitchen equipment. In addition, there should be separate spaces for goods storage, such as a larder, bulk store, dry goods store,

A comprehensive range of kitchen equipment in a large hostel.

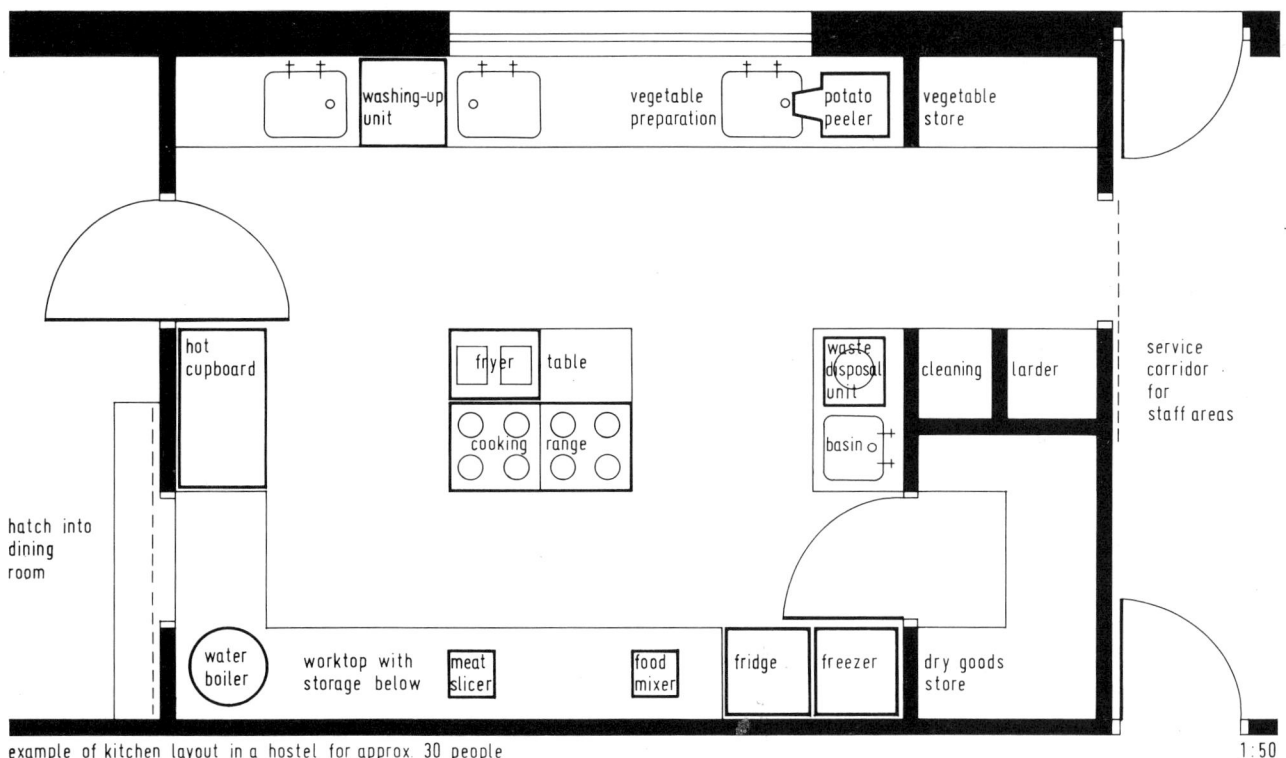

example of kitchen layout in a hostel for approx. 30 people

1:50

Housing for Single People, Shared Accommodation and Hostels

Staffed hostels presuppose the provision of a full catering service.

In very small hostels, a kitchen of domestic scale would be adequate.

vegetable store and cold store. A staff room and other ancillary accommodation may also be provided nearby.

3.5.21 Where meals are provided in this way from a single main kitchen, it would probably be inaccessible to residents for most of the time. Therefore, it would be desirable to include a small pantry fitted with a sink and minimal cooking facilities for each group of bed-sitting rooms or at least one on each floor of a large hostel.

3.5.22 In a self-catering hostel, where the residents are expected to provide their own meals, domestic kitchens together with some dining space and possibly a small sitting area should be provided separately for each group of bed-sitting rooms (see 3.5.4).

Small sitting area with each group of bed-sitting rooms.

Laundry

3.5.23 Laundries should be provided separately from kitchens. They should open off the hall or circulation areas rather than shared living spaces to avoid any nuisance caused by noise from washing machines. It is preferable for a heavy duty commercial-type washing machine and tumbler-dryer to be installed rather than domestic machines as the latter may not withstand heavy usage for very long. The commercial machines also generally have the advantage of working on shorter programmes. In addition to the machines, the laundry room should be equipped with a sink, worktop and storage cupboards, and space for ironing clothes with a suitably located power point. One of each of the main items, sink, washing machine and tumbler-dryer should be adequate for up to 30 people. Above that 2 of each

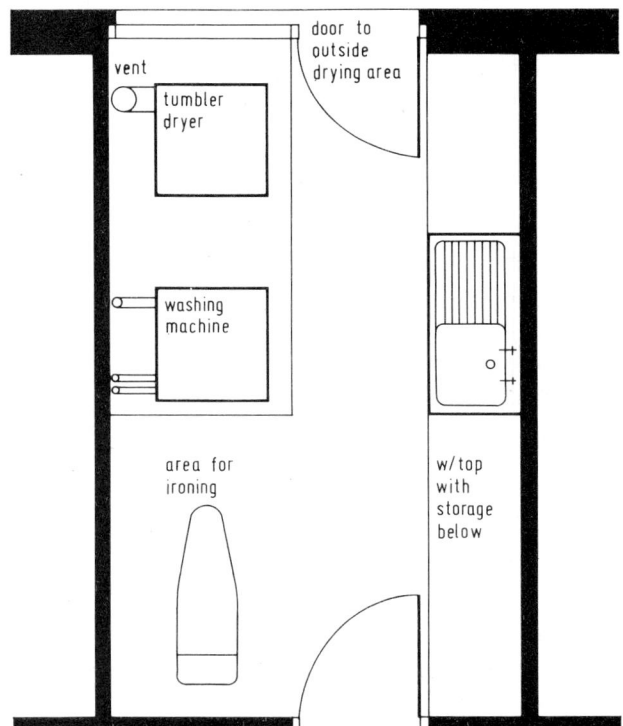
example of laundry layout in a hostel for approx. 30 people   1 : 50

should be provided. The laundry should be adequately ventilated at all times and tumbler-dryers must be separately vented to the outside. It is useful if the laundry can open directly onto an outside drying area.

Storage

3.5.24 Some general storage space should be provided with each group of bed-sitting rooms, but it would be necessary to have an additional store room centrally located, perhaps in association with the communal living area. A total volume of $3m^3$ per person should be adequate for general storage.

Storage space provided for each group of rooms.

Linen storage should also be provided centrally as residents are unlikely to launder their own bed linen. A cleaner's store could be provided either within the laundry space or close to it and should be equipped with a bucket sink at low level and a worktop and shelves alongside. In large hostels, a linen store and cleaner's store should be provided at each floor level. If necessary, some external storage space for gardening tools and other items should also be provided. Separate spaces will be provided for refuse storage.

Plant Rooms and Lifts

3.5.25 It is likely that a plant room will be required for the heating installation, and perhaps space for fuel storage, depending on the form of heating used. Consideration will need to be given to fire separation of these areas: access to them should be from the outside. A separate cupboard for electrical switchgear will also be required and this should be located near the main entrance. It should be remembered that in large hostels the space required for these functions may be extensive and detailed requirements rather elaborate. It is suggested that the advice of mechanical and electrical engineers be sought at an early stage in the design process in order to establish what provisions will be necessary.

3.5.26 Irrespective of the possible need to cater for elderly or disabled residents, lifts will always be provided in hostels more than four storeys high.

In large hostel developments, the space required for boiler rooms and other plant may be quite extensive.

A separate electrical switch room may also be necessary.

Parking

3.5.27 In hostels the need for car parking spaces for residents is likely to be rather limited (see 3.2.11). However, spaces should be provided for staff and visitors, and an unloading bay with manoeuvring space for delivery vans will also be required in association with the service areas. In large hostels particular attention should be given to the storage of refuse and provisions for its collection.

Optional Facilities

3.5.28 The following items are optional or additional facilities of which some may be considered desirable in certain circumstances. Many of these items are only appropriate in large hostels but some may be relevant in small hostels especially where there is a degree of resident care.

Housekeeper's Office

3.5.29 In large hostels, the organisation of catering, cleaning, maintenance and laundry work would probably be carried out by a housekeeper. A housekeeper's office could be provided in part of the service area, perhaps related to the central kitchen, or beside the staff sitting room. It should be furnished in similar fashion to the warden's office (see 3.5.14). The housekeeper's office should also be situated close to whichever entrance is used for goods deliveries, particularly for reception of items into the bulk storage areas of the kitchen.

Staff Sitting Room and Cloakroom

3.5.30 It may be necessary to provide a separate staff sitting room, together with a staff cloakroom and WC. The staff room may also accommodate a small dining area and it would be worthwhile if this was equipped with minimal cooking facilities. Another possibility would be to provide a small pantry nearby. This would be particularly useful if the warden or staff did not live in or very close to the development.

Duty Room

3.5.31 In schemes where it was anticipated that specialist care would be provided from outside, it would be desirable to provide a small day-staff duty room. In small hostels this function could probably be combined with a general staff room or the warden's office.

Hostels for Special Needs

3.5.32 Accommodation intended for elderly or disabled people will require some enhancement of space standards and/or heating standards, and other special design features (see 3.1.12–3.1.15).

3.5.33 Some types of hostel will be intended for occupation by elderly residents, of whom many may well be very frail. The additional space normally associated with accommodation for wheelchair users would be helpful to these residents because they often use walking aids, or have special types of furniture and other equipment (see 3.4.8).

3.5.34 Hostels for mentally handicapped people would not generally require any enhancement of space standards or special fittings unless the particular group of people to be housed also had physical disabilities. Some additional facilities may be needed such as an interview/treatment room or a hobbies room especially if the residents' degree of dependence requires a higher level of staffing, or if they are unable to go out to work.

Special Sanitary Facilities

3.5.35 In addition to the normal sanitary accommodation provided for each group of bed-sitting rooms, it may be necessary to include within the hostel special bathing facilities such as a large paraplegic bathroom with a peninsular bath for assisted bathing.

3.5.36 In some hostels, for instance those intended for frail elderly or disabled people, it may be necessary for at least some of the residents to be provided with separate individual sanitary facilities. This could open directly off the bed-sitting room and would be equipped with a shower, WC fitting, wash-hand basin and any grabrails or other fittings necessary for the assistance of the particular resident.

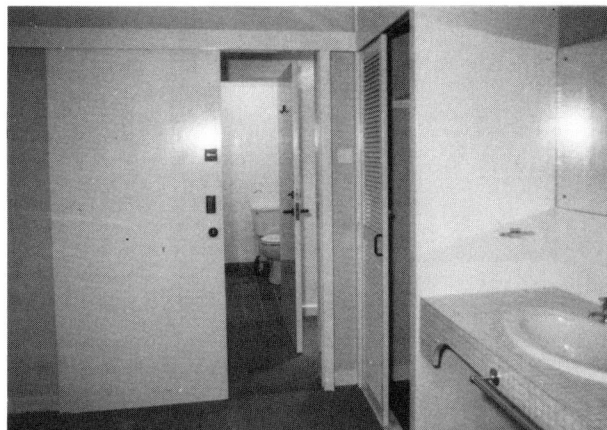

Disabled people may require separate sanitary facilities opening directly off their bed-sitting room.

3.5.37 Where severely disabled people are to be accommodated, a sluice room may be required for emptying and disposing of bed-pans etc.

3.5.38 In hostels specifically intended for wheelchair users, provision should be made for the charging of batteries on motor-driven wheelchairs. A separate well-ventilated room should be provided for this purpose, as the gases given off during the recharging process can be dangerous in a confined space.

Interview/Treatment Room

3.5.39 In hostels for physically disabled or mentally handicapped people it may be desirable to have a room for treating or interviewing residents, especially if the services of specialist staff are required. In some hostels these functions could be combined with a reception room beside the warden's office (see 3.5.16). The interview/treatment room should be large enough to contain a bed or couch, a desk and upright chair, and two easy chairs. It should also be fitted with a wash-hand basin or sink, worktop, shelves and a lockable medicine cupboard.

Hobbies Room

3.5.40 Some additional communal living space may be required for special needs groups to cater for the greater proportion of time spent on the premises. This could be either an extra sitting room, for instance in hostels for the elderly, or a separate hobbies room for younger disabled or mentally handicapped residents. Hobbies rooms should be equipped with some fitted storage units and worktops, and possibly a sink.

Guest Rooms

3.5.41 In hostels for special needs it would be desirable to provide a double bedroom to accommodate visiting friends or relatives. Built-in furniture and other fittings could be the same as for the residents' bed-sitters (see 3.4.9), but the shape of the room should permit the use of two single beds. Approximately one guest room should be sufficient for each twenty tenants. An extra WC and shower should adjoin the guest room and in large hostel schemes this could be shared by two or more rooms. It could also be shared with a staff bed-sitting room.

Accommodation for Staff

3.5.42 The warden's dwelling would normally consist of a three to five person house or flat designed to general needs housing standards. In some types of hostel, for example those for mentally handicapped people, it is desirable for the warden's house to blend in with the scheme. One possible way of achieving this would be to group the tenants' bed-sitting rooms and portions of the shared facilities into approximately dwelling-sized units. Two or three of these 'houses' could be linked together on the ground floor and constructed in the form of a short terrace, to which could be added a house of similar shell-size but of conventional internal layout for the warden. When the warden is provided with a flat then this should have its entrance separate from but possibly linked to the communal parts of the hostel. Whether the warden lives in a house or flat, it is desirable for some external space to be earmarked for the sole use of the warden's family.

3.5.43 In addition to the warden's dwelling, it may be necessary to provide accommodation for other residential staff, particularly in hostels for special needs. This might take the form of one or two person dwellings and it is likely that these would be included as an integral part of the hostel rather than as independent houses. Alternatively, bed-sitting rooms could be provided for resident staff. These could be similar in most respects to those occupied by the tenants, except that it would be preferable for them to have a separate WC and shower. Where two or more staff bed-sitting rooms are required, they could be placed close together so as to share the WC and shower. The guest room could be located nearby (see 3.5.41).

Warden's house attached to a small hostel of domestic scale and character.

3.6 ADAPTATIONS AND CONVERSIONS

Use of Existing Mainstream Dwellings

3.6.1 A significant contribution to the stock of shared housing is likely to come from the use of existing mainstream dwellings, and it is useful to consider which type and size of dwelling would be appropriate for this purpose (see 3.4.2). Typical family houses or flats are designed with one or two double bedrooms. Therefore, if each single person is to have a bedroom to himself, the dwellings would have to be under-occupied in relation to the total number of bedspaces available. In general, the simplest way of looking at this is to select dwellings where the number of apartments is at least one greater than the number of single people expected to occupy them. For example, a five person mainstream house would commonly be designed with four apartments. If this was converted for use as a shared dwelling, it would be suitable for three people. This principle is illustrated for other sizes of dwellings in Table 5 (see 3.1.4–3.1.10).

Tenement Buildings

3.6.2 Scottish cities are strongly characterised by extensive areas of four storey tenement buildings, mainly dating from the nineteenth century. Although much of the tenement stock is shabby in appearance, and in need of repair and modernisation, the basic structure of the building in many cases is sound. Moreover, rooms are frequently of pleasing proportions with many splendid Victorian decorative features such as marble fireplaces, moulded plaster cornices, panelled doors and other joinery of a quality of design and materials rarely encountered in housing today. Sensitive rehabilitation schemes which acknowledge these features can do much to preserve the character of the dwellings.

Nineteenth century tenement buildings often provide excellent opportunities for conversion to shared housing; the structure in many cases is sound and sensitive rehabilitation schemes can benefit from the Victorian decorative features.

3.6.3 Rehabilitation or improvement of these properties can be an effective way of providing shared accommodation for single people and can give a worthwhile new life to the older housing stock. Although access to top flats is inconvenient by modern standards, many young people are willing to climb three or four flights in a common stair for the sake of having their dwelling in a suitable location.

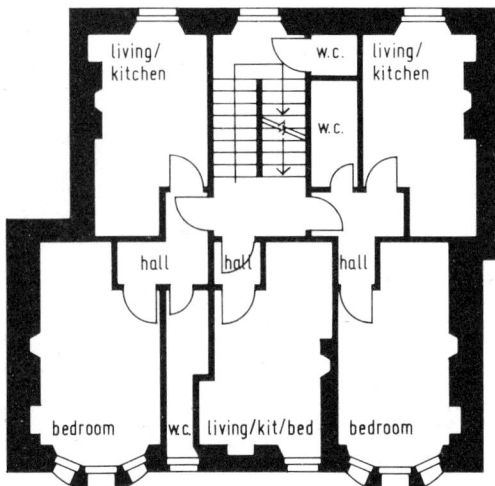

typical example of Glasgow tenement as existing

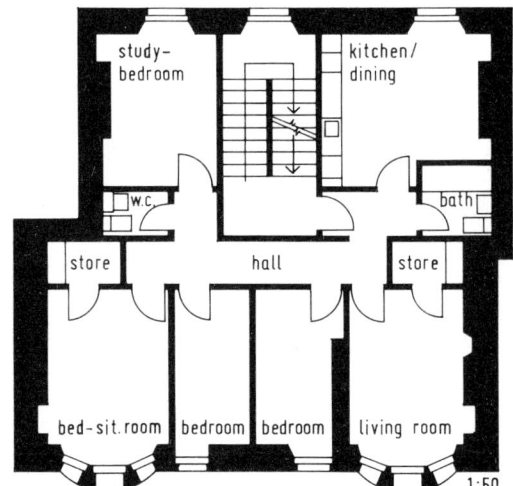

tenement altered to form 4-person shared dwelling

The inter-war housing stock may also provide opportunities for conversions.

Modern Walk-Up Flatted Developments

3.6.4 As with the nineteenth century tenements, modern walk-up flatted developments could readily be used to house groups of single people wishing to share a dwelling. Furthermore, in large developments a number of dwellings could be combined to form a hostel with some ground floor flats used to provide communal facilities and upper flats converted to groups of bed-sitting rooms. For instance, the four-person, three-apartment flat, which is very common, could be used in such a way that the two double bedrooms became two single bed-sits, the lounge became a double bed-sit and the kitchen was converted to a pantry with a small casual sitting area. On the other hand, if alterations to structure and service routes can be carried out reasonably easily, it may be possible to convert the larger dwellings into two or more one-person units.

High-Rise Buildings

3.6.5 Some housing authorities have made effective use of redundant multi-storey blocks of flats to provide sheltered or amenity housing for the elderly. Communal facilities have been added at ground level or provided by converting flats elsewhere in the building. A few examples already exist where similar conversions have been undertaken to provide housing for single people. However, with these forms of construction, it is likely that there will be problems associated with altering structures and service routes.

Converting Other Types of Building

3.6.6 Examples of other buildings which could be suitable for conversion to housing can be found among old warehouses or mills, where floor to floor heights are generally appropriate and where the external walls are often already punctuated at regular intervals with window openings. This makes such buildings particularly suitable for the cellular layout common in hostels, especially if a new core of shared facilities and circulation areas can be inserted into the centre of the building.

High-rise buildings no longer popular for families have sometimes been converted for single people.

Former industrial building re-used for housing including a number of one-person units.

3.6.7 When schemes of this kind are proposed consultations should take place at an early stage in the design process with the authorities responsible for statutory approvals arising from a change of use. For example, if the conversion is situated near to other old buildings, especially those of historic interest, care may well be needed in the treatment of external walls, new window openings and materials for re-covering the roof. Care may also need to be taken in the detailing of interiors where, for instance, existing iron columns or beams require additional fire protection.

Standards for Adaptations

3.6.8 Irrespective of what type of building is to be converted, designers should as far as possible aim to achieve standards of space and facilities equivalent to those for new-build (see 3.4.4). As rooms in old properties can sometimes be quite large, it would be sensible to use them as bed-sitting rooms rather than to divide them into smaller spaces suitable for bedrooms or study-bedrooms. In some cases it may be difficult to provide the full range of shared facilities associated with the standards for new-build. It is therefore recommended that a flexible attitude be adopted. For instance, more showers and less baths may be provided so that bathrooms can be fitted into existing structures, with the minimum disruption to partitions.

Conversion of older buildings may permit the inclusion of some large unfurnished bed-sits within existing generously sized rooms, for instance where elderly residents wish to bring furniture from previous homes.

Housing for Single People, Shared Accommodation and Hostels

4.1 APPLICATION OF STANDARDS

4.1.1 This section is intended to act as a checklist of those items which should be incorporated into the design of the different forms of accommodation for single people. The checklist should, so far as possible, be applied to converted existing buildings as well as new build schemes. Cross-references to paragraphs in the main text are included where relevant.

4.1.2 The recommendations listed as essential features are intended to cover the basic provisions required to fulfil the definitions of the three types of housing, *one-person housing, shared housing* and *hostels*. They are not exhaustive and there may be other features to be considered.

4.1.3 Optional features appropriate to each are listed separately. Although not essential to fulfil the basic definitions they may be considered for inclusion in large schemes or where special needs are to be catered for. Reference should be made to Scottish Housing Handbook, Part 5: 'Housing for the Elderly' and Part 6: 'Housing for the Disabled' which contain detailed recommendations intended to cater for these groups.

4.2 ONE-PERSON HOUSING

Essential Features

4.2.1 The design of one-person dwellings should in every respect be in accordance with the standards for general needs housing, and should fulfil all the requirements of the Building Regulations for buildings in occupancy sub-groups A1 or A2.

1. One-apartment dwellings should have a gross floor area not less than $32.5m^2$ for flats or $33.0m^2$ for houses. (2.5.4–8, 3.1.2, 3.3.2).
2. Two-apartment dwellings should have a gross floor area not less than $37m^2$. (2.5.4–8, 3.1.2., 3.3.3).
3. The gross floor areas for each type include areas for living, sleeping, dining, kitchen, bathroom, general storage, linen store, internal circulation and partitions. (2.5.8, 3.1.3–9, 3.3.4–6).

Optional Features

4.2.2 The following additional facilities may be considered desirable in some developments.

1. In schemes catering for special needs, some enhancement of space and/or heating standards, and other special design features may be necessary. (3.1.12–15).
2. One car parking space for every three residents. (3.2.8–14).
3. Communal laundry containing sinks, commercial standard washing-machines and tumbler-dryers, one of each for every 30 tenants. (3.3.8).
4. Small, late-opening shop. (3.3.9).
5. Communal lounge area, $0.5m^2$ per tenant ($20m^2$ min.), with a pantry, cloakroom and WC, and public telephone near to the main entrance. (3.3.10–12).
6. Cleaner's store for communal circulation areas. (3.3.13).
7. Plant room and electrical switch room. (3.3.14).
8. Office and/or a 3–5 person mainstream dwelling for a caretaker. (3.3.15–17).
9. Entry-phone system. (3.3.18).

4.3 SHARED HOUSING

Essential Features

4.3.1 The design of shared dwellings should be in accordance with the standards prescribed in the Building Regulations for buildings in occupancy sub-groups A1 or A2. The essential distinguishing features are as follows.

1. Purpose designed shared dwellings should have a gross floor area per person not less than that indicated in Table 5. (2.5.9–13, 3.4.2).
2. Ordinary mainstream housing shared by single people should have a number of apartments at least one greater than the number of occupants. (2.5.9–13, 3.4.3–4).
3. The private space for each person would normally be a study-bedroom (10m² minimum). Exceptionally, a double study-bedroom (16m² minimum) might be included. (3.1.2, 3.4.5–7).
4. The shared space includes living room, dining area, kitchen, bathroom and WC, general storage, linen store, internal circulation and partitions. (2.5.13, 3.1.3–9, 3.4.11).
5. The dining area would normally be combined with the kitchen, or the main shared living space may be a large farmhouse kitchen. (3.4.12–13).
6. The design of the kitchen should permit the inclusion of larger or additional items of equipment, and storage space for each person. Part of the kitchen may be in a separate utility room. (3.4.14–15).
7. In shared dwellings for four or more people a second WC fitting is required, and for six or more a second bath/shower fitting, as shown in Table 8. (3.4.16–17).
8. The volume of general storage should provide 3m³ minimum for each person. (3.4.18).
9. Grade I standards of sound insulation to be provided between private rooms and shared areas, and in the partitions and floors separating the private rooms from one another. (3.4.19–21).
10. The private space should be heated to the same level as living rooms. (3.4.22).
11. Each private room should have 3 double power sockets (4 in double rooms). (3.4.23–24).

Optional Features

4.3.2 The following additional facilities may be considered desirable in some developments.

Items 1–9 as for One-Person Housing. (4.2.2).
10. Fitted and fixed furniture within each private space, such as a lockable wardrobe, drawers, desk, shelving, and possibly a vanitory unit. (3.4.8–10).

4.4 HOSTELS

Essential Features

4.4.1 The design of hostels should be in accordance with the standards prescribed in the Building Regulations for buildings in occupancy sub-group A3. (Certain types of residential homes for special needs may be classified A4.) The essential distinguishing features are as follows.

1. Hostels should have a gross floor area per person not less than that indicated in Table 6. (2.5.14–18, 3.5.2).
2. Hostels will usually be staffed and designed so as to be capable of providing a full catering service. Alternatively, they may sometimes be self-catering hostels, with limited staffing and where no meals are provided. (2.5.14–18, 3.5.2–4).
3. The private space for each person would normally be a bed-sitting room (13m² minimum). Exceptionally a small proportion of double bed-sitting rooms (19m² minimum) might be included. (3.4.5.–7, 3.5.5).
4. The shared space includes communal living areas, warden's office, bathrooms, WCs, kitchen, larder and other kitchen stores, pantries, laundry room, cleaner's stores, linen stores, general storage, external storage, plant rooms, entrance hall, corridors, ducts, partitions and staircases. (2.5.18, 3.1.3.–10, 3.5.6).
5. The living areas would be a common room, with dining area linked to the kitchen with a hatch or servery. In larger hostels, it is desirable for separate spaces to be provided for lounge, TV room, and dining. (3.5.7–10).
6. A cloakroom with separate male and female WCs should be provided off the main entrance hall. (3.5.11).
7. The common room, cloakrooms and other 'public areas' should be accessible for the disabled. (3.5.12).
8. A warden's office should be provided close to the main entrance together with a small reception area and a public telephone. (3.5.13–17).
9. At least one bath or shower and one WC should be provided for every 5 occupants, as shown in Table 9. (3.5.18–19).
10. The main kitchen should be designed to provide a full catering service, with a comprehensive range of kitchen equipment, and separate spaces for storage including larder, bulk store and cold store. (3.5.20–22).
11. A small pantry should be provided for each group of bed-sitting rooms. (3.5.21).
12. The laundry should be equipped with sinks, commercial standard washing machines and tumbler-dryers, one of each to every 30 occupants. (3.5.23).

---

13. General storage should be provided with each group of bed-sitting rooms, 3m³ per person. The linen store and cleaner's store should be provided centrally. An external store and a separate refuse store will also be necessary. (3.5.24).
14. Separate spaces will be necessary for an electrical switch room and plant room. Fuel storage may be required. (3.5.25).
15. Detailed design considerations regarding sound attenuation, heating appliances and power points should be the same as for shared housing. (3.4.19–25, 4.3.1 items 9–11).

Optional Features

4.4.2 The following additional facilities may be considered desirable in some hostels.

1. Fitted and fixed furniture within each private space such as a lockable wardrobe, drawers, desk, shelving, and possibly a vanitory unit. (3.4.8–10).
2. A lift may be necessary to cater for elderly or disabled tenants and must be included if the hostel is more than 4 storeys high. (3.5.26).
3. Space for parking or garaging of cars and bicycles. (3.5.27).
4. Housekeeper's office. (3.5.29).
5. Domestic staff sitting room, with cloakroom and WC. (3.5.30).
6. Duty room for visiting day-care staff. (3.5.31).
7. In schemes catering for special needs, some enhancement of space and/or heating standards and other special design features may be necessary. (3.1.12–15, 3.5.32–34).
8. Special sanitary facilities, such as a paraplegic bathroom, individual WC/shower rooms, and a sluice room. (3.5.35–37).
9. Battery charging room for wheelchairs. (3.5.38).
10. Additional communal living areas eg a hobbies room. (3.5.40).
11. Guest room and WC. (3.5.41).
12. House or flat designed to mainstream housing standards for the warden. (3.5.42).
13. Accommodation for staff in the form of small flats, or bed-sitting rooms sharing a WC/shower room. (3.5.43).

BIBLIOGRAPHY

Housing of Special Groups: A Report by the Scottish Housing Advisory Committee, HMSO 1952.

Residential Accommodation for Staff, Hospital Building Note 24, Ministry of Health, London, HMSO 1964.

Metric Space Standards, New Scottish Housing Handbook Bulletin 1, SDD, HMSO 1968.

Housing Single People 1: How they live at present, DOE Design Bulletin 23, HMSO 1971.

Housing Single People 2: A Design Guide with a Description of a Scheme at Leicester, DOE Design Bulletin 29, HMSO 1974.

Housing for Single Young People: A Study Related to the Demand for Existing Housing Stock, Raper, Research Paper 7, Institute of Advanced Architectural Studies, York 1974.

House Conversions for Students, Goodey Matthew and Lyon, Research Paper 3, Institute of Advanced Architectural Studies, York 1974.

Housing and Social Work, a Joint Approach: The Report of the Morris Committee on Links between Housing and Social Work, SDD, HMSO 1975.

Small Group Homes and Group Homes for Adults, Check Lists of Accommodation Nos 5 and 6, issued to Regional Authorities by SED (SWSG) 1975.

Housing for Single Young People: A Survey of Single Young People Living in Multi-Occupied Houses, Chippindale, Research Paper 11, Institute of Advanced Architectural Studies, York 1976.

Hostels and Lodgings for Single People, Digby, Office of Population Censuses and Surveys, HMSO 1976.

Housing for the Single Person, Discussion Paper ST2/2, Scottish Local Authorities Special Housing Group, Edinburgh 1976.

Residential Homes for the Elderly, Social Work Building Note 2, SED (SWSG), Edinburgh 1976.

Housing for Single Young People: The Design and Adaptation of Existing House Types for Shared Use, Edmonds, Research Paper 12, Institute of Advanced Architectural Studies, York 1977.

Scottish Housing Handbook, Part 1: Assessing Housing Needs, SDD, HMSO 1977.

Scottish Housing Handbook, Part 3: Housing Development: Layout, Roads and Services, SDD, HMSO 1977.

Single Person Housing, Part 1: Needs and Provisions and Part 2: Projects, Case Study 6, Housing Rehabilitation Handbook pp 1143–1150 and pp 1237–1242, Architects Journal 15 June and 29 June 1977.

Housing Single People 3: An Appraisal of a Purpose-Built Scheme, DOE Design Bulletin 33, HMSO 1978.

The Housing Needs of Single People and the Use of Older Properties, Hole and Taylor, Building Research Establishment, 1978.

Not Only . . . But Also: A Report on Shared Housing for Single People, Wainwright, Scottish Council for Single Homeless, Edinburgh 1979.

Conversion for Single Persons: A Report to the Housing Corporation, NBA, Edinburgh 1979.

Scottish Housing Handbook, Part 6: Housing for the Disabled, SDD, HMSO 1979.

Brief for the Single Person: Design and Management Issues, Scottish Council for Single Homeless, Edinburgh 1980.

Survey of Hostels and Lodging Houses in Scotland, pp 5–13, Scottish Housing Statistics No 8 4th Quarter 1979, SDD, HMSO 1980.

Changing Patterns of Care: Report on Services for the Elderly in Scotland, SHHD and SED (SWSG), HMSO 1980.

Scottish Housing Handbook, Part 5: Housing for the Elderly, SDD, HMSO 1980.

Single Initiatives I: A Study of Single Person and Special Needs Housing by Housing Associations, Currie, Scottish Council for Single Homeless, Edinburgh 1980.

Housing for Mentally Handicapped People, Heginbotham, National Society for Mentally Handicapped Children and Adults, London 1980.

Residential Care Research Review: A Review of Published Literature on the Viability of Small Residential Units for Mentally Handicapped People, and Factors Involved in the Development of Non-Institutional Care, McKnight, Thomas Coram Research Unit, University of London Institute of Education, London 1980.

Housing (Homeless Persons) Act 1977: Code of Guidance—Scotland, SDD 1980.

Housing for Single Young People: Cluster Dwellings for Housing Association Tenants: A Development Project Using Existing Buildings, Edmonds, Research Paper 18, Institute of Advanced Architectural Studies, York 1981.

Think Single: An Assessment of the Accommodation Experiences, Needs and Preferences of Single People, Buchanan, Balmer and Blaikie, Scottish Council for Single Homeless, Edinburgh 1981.

Single Initiatives II: Planning and Building, Currie, Scottish Council for Single Homeless, Edinburgh 1981.

Shared Housing for Single People, Wirz, Raitt, Wilson and MacMillan, University of Edinburgh, Scottish Office Central Research Unit Papers, Edinburgh 1982.

Housing Initiatives for Single People of Working Age, Adams *et al,* DOE London 1982.

ACKNOWLEDGEMENTS

The Scottish Development Department wish to thank the Convention of Scottish Local Authorities, the Scottish Federation of Housing Associations, the Scottish Special Housing Association, the New Towns/SSHA Joint Working Party, the Housing Corporation, the Institute of Housing (Scottish Branch), the Royal Incorporation of Architects in Scotland, the Association of Chief Architects of Scottish Local Authorities, the Scottish Local Authorities Special Housing Group, and the Scottish Council for Single Homeless, who contributed valuable comments upon the discussion paper entitled 'Housing for Single People, Shared Accommodation and Hostels' which was circulated by SDD during 1982 and upon which Scottish Housing Handbook Part 7 is based.

Special acknowledgement is made of assistance received from housing agencies, authorities and associations, building professionals and residents of housing developments studied during preparation of this part of the Handbook. Much useful information has been received from discussions with the many bodies and individuals actively promoting, providing, designing, building and occupying housing for single people.

Thanks for permission to reproduce illustrations are due to the following:

Philip Cocker and Partners (Architects) and A L Hunter (Photographer)

Wheeler and Sproson (Architects)

Whitedael Housing Association

Scottish Special Housing Association and H Thomson (Photographer) and H Snoek (Photographer)

Edinvar Housing Association and S Guthrie (Photographer)

Norman Raitt, Architecture Research Unit and S Guthrie (Photographer)

Ian H Rolland and Partners (Architects)

City of Edinburgh District Council Planning Department

Salvation Army Housing Association and Walker and Scott (Architects)

Printed in the UK for HMSO
Dd 735850 C20 7/84 (4458) (13129)

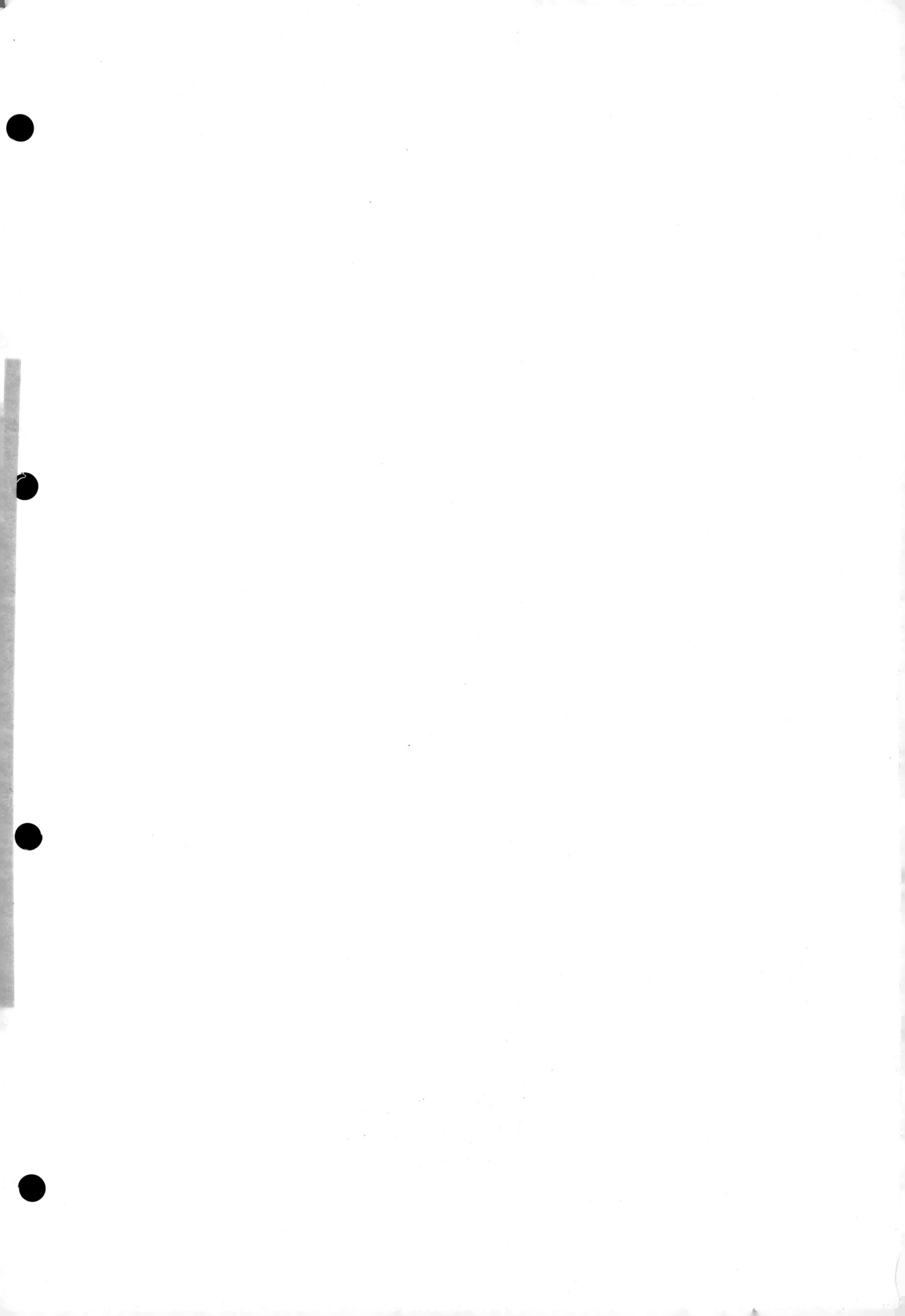

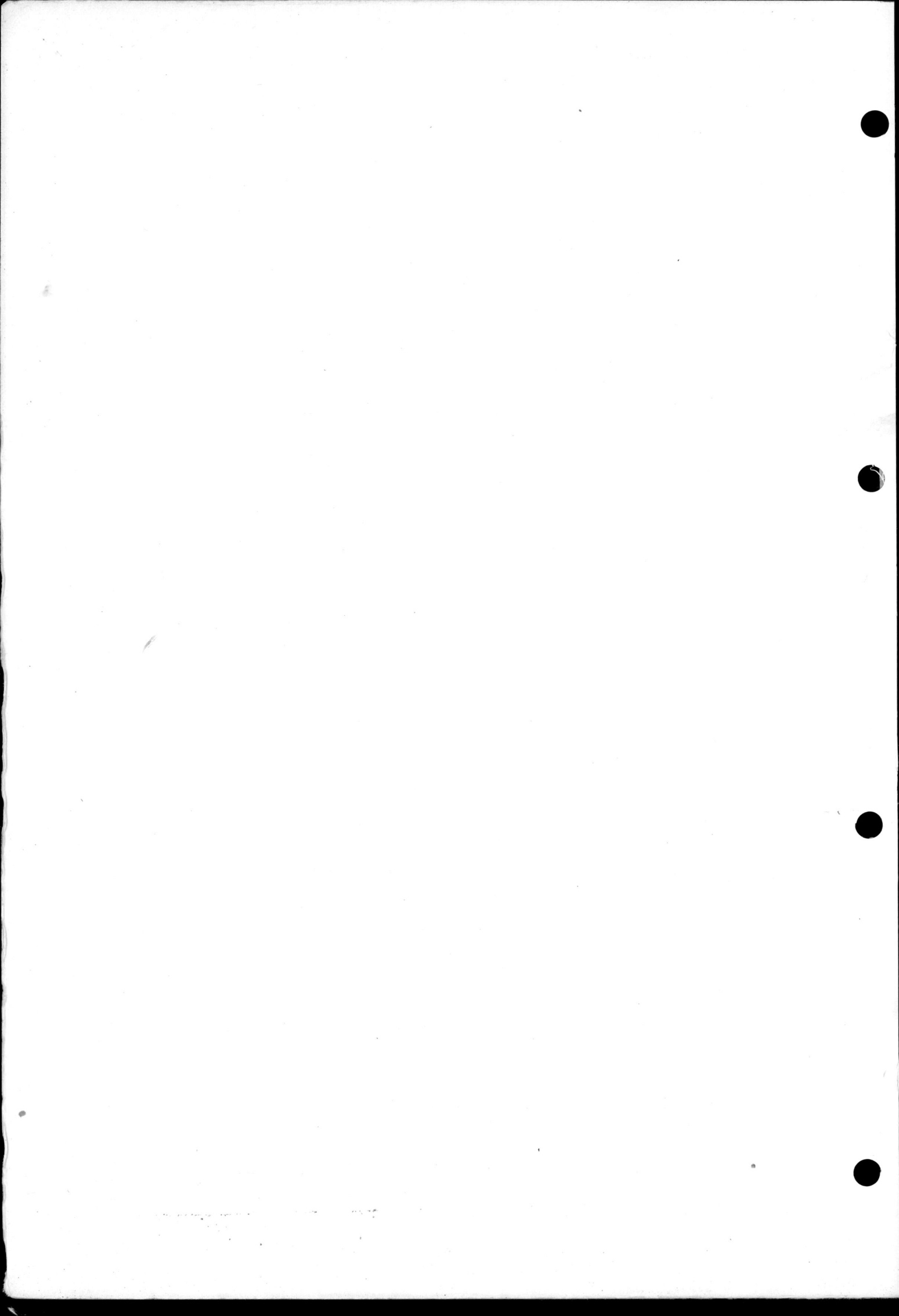